On Jericho Flats

A NOVEL

MARK DUFF

Copyright © 2021 by Mark Duff

ISBN (paperback): 978-0-578-95309-0
ISBN: (ebook): 978-0-578-95312-0

Grateful acknowledgment is made to Ben Way, Doreen Martens, cover photo: Mark Duff, cover design: Jack Elder, back cover photo, chapter photo, and last photo: Mark Duff, drawings: Tish McFee, author photo: Elijah Pettet, design: Euan Monaghan

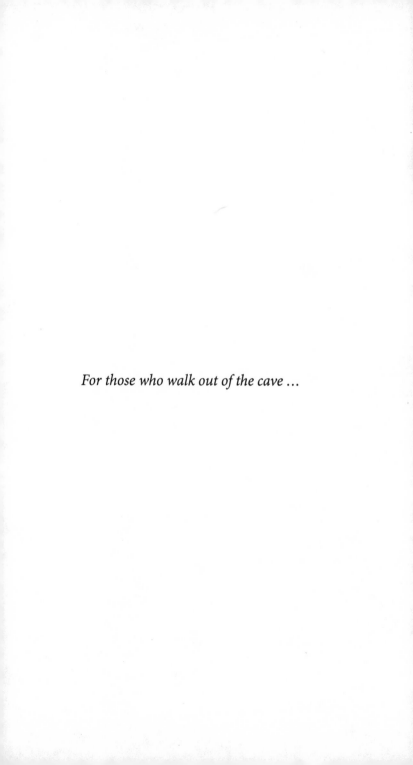

For those who walk out of the cave …

CHAPTER ONE

Every blade of grass has meaning ...

A Raven soars high and free over an Aspen Forest high up in the Colorado Rockies. The bird lets out a guttural croak as it glides over the top of the puffy green canopy. The Raven sees the leaves and branches roll by as it feels the cool air on its feathers. The forest is real for the bird, and the connection is intimate, like a familiar friend.

The Tree, the Grove, the Forest—shaded and cool, green and breezy with trembling leaves; all is crisp and frozen white-on-white during the long, deep winter. Its roots entangled in the jumbled debris of an ancient glacial moraine. Eyes that look out, black and squinting, from the white bark, keep watch from a point in time and space. Consciousness held within the lore of the mountain.

From the creek on the valley floor, the Aspen Forest climbs up the southwest slope, struggling to find purchase in the treacherous moraine. Here, when the glaciers retreated, a tenacious lone seed drifted on the air until it found a viable spot, and in that moment, the very moment, it slowly germinated and then sprouted. Growing, waxing, and waning over the centuries and millennia, multiplying and marching across the landscape. Buff-white tree trunks, ancient, decaying, and falling, only to re-sprout and thrive. The forest moved upward during warm spells, then receded down to the valley floor when it was cold. Expanding, receding, burning, and re-sprouting, again and again. A living expression of the amplitude of time, to have always been here, here in the eternal present, a witness, right at the very edge of its unfolding; a sentinel both feeling and knowing.

There in the creek, the water sings; the Raven flies. To see through its eyes, feel the wind on shimmering silver-black wings that stretch all the way to the horizon. Squint your eyes and enter a dream.

* * *

A Raven flies effortlessly hundreds of feet above the University of Colorado campus. The big black bird turns its head and looks down at the maroon-red tile roofs and red sandstone buildings. It glides on an invisible stream of air that blows heavy over the continental divide of the Rocky Mountain front some 50 miles to the west.

Jake exits the university lecture hall through the tall, heavy doors into the campus's open central quad. It is late spring, and he stands there in his shorts and T-shirt, surveying the courtyard; the grass is green and the large elm trees sway in the breeze. He is tall and muscular from spending his free time rock-climbing and running the mountain trails around Boulder. Young people are sprawled on the lawn where Frisbees fly and students roll by on bicycles and skateboards. He stands on the concrete steps looking around for Isabella. He spots her walking through the dappled light as if she's floating; she is wearing a summer dress and strolling barefoot with her sandals in her hand. They smile when they catch each other's eyes. Jake jumps down the steps and they embrace. She leans back in his arms and brushes her dark hair back, and says, "We're done!"

Jake responds with equal enthusiasm, "I can't believe it, that was my last final. Done!"

They lie down in the shade of an elm. Jake rests his head on his backpack, and Isabella has her head on Jake's shoulder. He says, "Ah, there's a million things to do before the folks get here for all the graduation stuff."

Isabella replies with a smile, "Yeah, I've got to pick up my cap and gown and check out of my zoo-lab."

Jake rolls over to face her. "How about I make us dinner tonight? You know, something nice."

"I'd love that." He reaches over and playfully pulls on the edge of her dress. "Stop that! It's the middle of campus." Jake flashes a big smile, groans, and rolls over on his back. He points up to the brilliant blue Colorado sky. "Look, see the birds flying so high up?"

"Where?"

"There, up high, like a hundred feet. Way off the deck. Looks like Ravens, I think ..." he says, pointing and following the big black birds gliding silently.

Isabella smiles, rolls over, and kisses him. "You notice all these little things as they pass by."

Jake watches the birds heading west and says, "Those birds can see everything from up there. Wouldn't it be cool if we could fly and see what they see?"

Changing the subject, Isabella asks, "So after graduation, we're going to head out and camp up there, you know, at Jericho, right?"

"Yeah, it's still on. You're okay with it all, yeah?"

Isabella reaches out and gently touches Jake's curly hair. "Yeah, but explain it to me again. What happened up there?"

Jake stirs, sits up, and, almost as if it were a confession, starts talking. "It all started that last day of fourth grade. But really, that wasn't it. No, it was at Jericho Flats, on our camping trip when I was a kid. That's where it all happened."

Isabella looks back at Jake with concern in her eyes and says, "But you're so smart. You double-majored in biology and philosophy, plus all those classes in physics or quantum-whatever. Babe, you can do anything. Why this?"

Jake quietly stares out at the courtyard, then looks up and tries to spot the birds again. "You know, we all are just so over-connected with our technology. We have to recognize the pathos that these e-devices represent. All of us are helpless in the face of these things. Yeah, but really, it did happen. I saw it, and we talked—well, we communicated. Anyway, I can see now that there is only one way."

"Is it about your grandfather?"

"No, that's just a part of it. He's gone, after all; he died that year. But no, it's more about nature, the natural world. I spent my entire childhood in the woods, walking around, exploring, enjoying nature, just free—free to observe and move. And now it's pretty much gone, and everyone is living a life of illusion—and that's no life." Jake sits up and looks around the quad. "I keep thinking about my dad. The way he would just stand there at the glass door and watch the birds—silent, like a statue. He'd watch every bird like it meant something."

Isabella runs her hand down Jake's arm and grabs his hand. "Look around. We're the only ones not staring at a screen or on a Scion." They glance at the other young people, most of whom are watching a holographic image floating above a Scion, a device that looks like an ordinary pair of wire-rim glasses. In their minds, a glowing image is cast. Other students stretch out on the grass and stare into their phone or laptop or tablet screen, oblivious to their surroundings.

Jake rolls his eyes and points. "Look at the Twitchers." Isabella gazes over at the individuals in hooded red robes, each wearing a Scion, their bodies slightly twitching as their hands move in spastic gestures. Jake looks at them with disdain. "So content in The Order, set to complacency as servants to the AI. You know, they never even see the Machine, just an illusion of what It presents to them. That way it's easier for them to believe." Jake remembers almost joining The Order himself.

He was in Professor Harold's office, debating a question on the last test. The professor said, "Jake, you have got to decide what you want to do. You are one of the brightest students I have ever had. Here, I've written you a letter of recommendation to join The Order of the Scion. I have sent it to your email. I want you to apply." Jake felt a wave of reservation and trepidation in his chest. It felt like every muscle was trembling. There was a distinct loss of words. Mumbling, he responded, "Well … thank you, I'll consider it. But really, they do what they do for a belief. I do it for what is real—for knowledge." The professor seemed displeased with this response; he had a perplexed look on his face. But Jake knew better; he had seen the Forest and the Machine and understood they were mutually exclusive.

He turns to Isabella and says, "It is our responsibility; some things are bigger than us." She picks up a dark-green elm leaf and twirls it in her hand. Jake takes it from her and says, "Here, I'll explain. You see, I can take this three-dimensional leaf—the 'real leaf'—and represent it in two dimensions by making a drawing." He reaches into his backpack, grabs a notebook, and quickly flips the pages open. He places the leaf under a sheet of paper and streaks over it with a pencil. The carbon moves quickly back and forth on the paper over the leaf, and a perfect image emerges, complete with details of the serrated edges, the exact number of serrations, and the rough venation.

"But," he continues, "I can also project a hologram of the leaf here with the Scion." Jake reaches into his pack and extracts his device. He touches its edge and a holographic projection of the leaf floats above it. Jake touches the hologram, so the hologram of the leaf expands and enlarges. Then he flicks the leaf-image and it rotates lazily in the air. "So, there's the leaf, the drawing, and the hologram. But which is the 'real leaf'?" He playfully takes the pencil and hikes up the edge of Isabella's dress. She slaps his hand and smiles at him. Jake continues, "But it really might be that all of this, our reality, might just be a three-dimensional projection, like the leaf-image hologram, from a faraway two-dimensional world."

Warming to the subject, he says, "And remember how in the quantum realm, the world smaller than an atom, particles can be entangled, yes? That's how the AI Machine communicates with the Scions."

Isabella perks up and says, "Yeah, it's like the 'spooky action at a distance' thing, right?"

"Yes, you got it. You can have two particles move and behave in the exact same way, regardless of the space between them. For example, a photon here on campus can move to the left, and on the other side of the planet another photon will move exactly the same. Or, for that matter, on the other side of the universe, because they are entangled."

Isabella looks up, wrinkles her nose, and says, "But what about the very end of the—"

Jake cuts her off. "We can't see it, but the evidence is there. The edge of the universe can and will only exist in our minds."

"That's because the light from there hasn't reached us yet."

Jake smiles, nods his head, and pushes his hair back. "And remember, it all hinges on the fact that each particle has a twin antiparticle. So, if a particle and an antiparticle come together, they annihilate each other. It was back then; it all unfolded at that time." He touches the Scion and an image of a curly-haired, blond boy floats above it.

Isabella smiles and laughs, "Oh, you were such a cute kid!"

Jake smiles and says, "You remember how it was, back in grade school on those last days of the school year? It was either playing games outside or on a Scion, doing one last assignment." He looks across the quad at a squirrel hopping up to the base of a large tree. He remembers how he spent most of the fourth grade staring out of the window. *He would just watch the squirrels feeding in the honey locust trees, tearing up the large dark-brown "bean pods" in the fall and winter, and eating the leaf buds in the spring.* Jake leans back and gazes at the blue sky, recalling those days. Isabella curls back on his shoulder. "Back then, 12 years ago, I was 10 years old. And it happened on that camping trip. There, at Jericho Flats. You know, the Aspen Forest is real, and it does have a voice."

* * *

Jake is in fourth grade, seated at a desk by the window. He is gazing out at the schoolyard, watching a squirrel in the honey locust tree, with its bright-green leaves swaying in the spring breeze. The boy is daydreaming about going camping during the coming summer break. He walks under an immense sky, alive and free. It is a genuine, unbounded feeling of joy. Seated at her desk in the front of the class, the teacher looks up and scolds him. "Now, Jake—let's get to work."

"But can't we go out and play?"

"No, you have to finish one last journal entry."

"But are you really going to grade these?" he asks plaintively.

With a stern look on her face, she says, "Jake, I'm crazy-busy here getting the grades done. And you know that both the computer and I review your assignments." Floating in front of the teacher is a hologram of a spreadsheet of students' names and their grades. She reaches out and scrolls down the gossamer screen. "I would like you to connect with your Scion and finish your CNav journal entry." Jake glumly fires up the device and launches the career computer program used by all the students. The teacher continues, "Please login and answer the CNav questions. The program will help you in your future career."

Jake takes one last look out the window and focuses on his Scion. His hands start to move as if he were writing on a whiteboard. His cheek muscles twitch slightly. The other 23 pupils in the room are also wearing Scions and wiggling away. Unknown to the young boy, the Machine integrates electrical signals with neurons as it directly communicates within the recesses of Jake's brain. In his mind's eye, he sees a brilliant, glowing blue; not something frightening, but soothing, like a warm blanket wrapped around him. And it comes— always awake, continually moving—like a shark, deep and relentless. It asks him about what he wants. Jake perceives the communique as a voice that's not really a voice, but more like an echo in his head. Jake explains: *It would be nice to be driving a real fast, red sports car on a winding road overlooking the ocean.* But there's something more. He sees a reddish flame and hears a rhythmic thumping sound. Jake says in his mind: *I can see you.* And the reddish-orange light spins around and says, *What? What is this trespass? You're not supposed to see me!* The sound reverberates; thump, thump, thump.

The teacher and the kids both know that the AI computer will evaluate the students by the number of assignments they complete and the time spent on their Scions doing so. Her evaluation will be a measure of the students' engagement through the device. At the end of the day, she stands in front of the class, saying goodbye at the close of term. "Now, you all have a great summer break. Remember that grades don't go in until Monday, so you can upload some more CNav journal entries to boost my … I mean, *your* grade."

CHAPTER TWO

The next morning, Jake's dad, Whitman Albright, lies in bed listening to the noisy trill of bird song. He turns and looks at the clock—5:47 a.m.—and thinks, *Might as well get up; the alarm will go off shortly. The birds sure are making a racket, probably the peak of June's mating quest.* He identifies one of the bird calls as a red-winged blackbird. *I better get ready for the meeting.* His thoughts are interrupted by the alarm's beeping, and he reaches over to turn it off so his wife, Judy, can sleep a little longer. Whit stands and looks out of the open bedroom window and feels the crisp, early morning air. The mornings are always fresh here in western Colorado. He can see that the high peaks still have snow on them. In the morning light, the snow stands out brightly against the green canopy and blue sky, in what is spring in the Rocky Mountains. The high-country snow is an off-reddish-white, stained by the dust blowing in from the deserts to the west. The discolored snow is occurring more often as spring storms are now more wind than snow. As Whit exits the bedroom, a black and white dog emerges from the other room and circles his feet.

* * *

Up-valley from Whit's small suburban house is a cattail marsh resonating with the trilling come-hither calls of red-winged blackbirds. A male perches on the end of a cattail stalk in the center of the wetland, and the dry stem bends and sways slightly under the weight of the bird. The cattails are a light brown, tangled mass of crisscrossed leaf blades and old seed head stalks. The bird sticks his wings out, flares the bright-red epaulet feathers, and spreads its tail feathers. At the base of each red feather is a tiny muscle that makes it flash erect. The bird drops his head and sends a boasting, raucous call in the direction of another male. In response, its chest swells and lets out an extended call and display back. The first bird has secured the prime, central nesting territory in the marsh and intends to defend his patch. He has six females on various nests in the tangled, overlapping vegetation. Most of the eggs in these nests are his offspring. He has risked it all to obtain this territory. He arrived in the early spring, having endured the migration here, then the snowstorms and the limited food available at that time of the year.

Spread throughout the cattail marsh are a dozen-plus other male birds on lesser territories, with fewer females on nests. At the edge of the marsh, near the bike path, is another male with only one female. Even further out, toward the irrigation ditch on the other side of the bike path, is an immature first-year, calling away. He has no female and only an empty, half-built nest. The young bird is a dull brownish-black with scarcely visible red on his wings—he sways on the end of a dead willow branch and calls and calls in vain.

The Sun peeks over the eastern ridge and the long morning light streaks across the valley floor. At that moment, the birds change their calls, fidget, look around, and all at once take flight. The flock takes a direct route that follows the bike path into the town to forage.

* * *

Morning sunlight streams through the sliding-glass door as Whitman sits at the kitchen table sipping his coffee and looking out into the backyard at the birds squabbling on the feeders. A flock of red-winged blackbirds has descended en masse. There is a cacophony of trilling song and flashing red-wing feathers. Mixed in with the blackbirds are a few cowbirds. In the apple tree, at the suet feeder, the starlings and magpies are noisily competing for the food. Tippers, the black and white herding dog, lies at Whit's feet. He waits calmly, with his front legs crossed, watching the birds. Whit stands up and ambles slowly to refill his coffee cup. Tippers jumps up and quickly circles his feet and does a quick, strike-like bite at Whit's fur-lined moccasins. The dog looks up at the man, then runs to the glass door, circles, and looks back. Whit looks at him and says, "It's early; everyone is still sleeping." Then Whit shakes his head and relents to the dog's enthusiastic demand and opens the door. Tipper's claws scrape the frame as he launches out into the yard. He chases the birds in a set of leaps and bounds and gives off a slight, grunting bark. Thwarted, he then circles the backyard and finishes with a spinning leap at the base of a chokecherry tree. He play-bows while looking up at the birds in the tree, rump in the air and his tail wagging; then he launches straight up with a sharp-sounding bark.

Judy walks up behind Whit and puts her hand and chin on her husband's shoulder, saying, "You're just making him crazier than he already is. Call him in now; he'll wake up the neighbors." Whit slides the back door open and whistles. The dog runs in and circles around Judy's feet, while looking up and soliciting a few pats on the head along with a loving scolding. "You are a bad dog, Tips! You got to be quiet now," she says. The dog drops his ears and wags his tail.

Whit stands at the sliding glass door, looking at the birds reassembling around the feeders. He says, "Should I wake Jake? I really want to get started."

Judy is scrolling on her phone and replies, "No, not yet. He only finished school yesterday." With a couple of quick taps on the phone screen, the radio turns on.

Whit nods, all the while looking at the birds. "Okay, I'll finish packing the food."

"How many days are you going to be up there?"

Whit sipped his coffee and swallowed. "Oh, three, I guess. We'll be back Monday, as I have to be in the office on Tuesday. I wish you could join us."

Judy replies, "Next time. I've got too much going on with work. Besides, it's good for you guys to have a boys' trip."

Judy unfolds what looks like an ordinary pair of wire-rim glasses and places them on the kitchen counter. "And your dad is already up there?" A hologram floats above the device and starts off with a colorful advertisement for the new Scion-5. An attractive young woman with an Australian accent explains about the new device. *It's out now and available for you! Just roll over to a brand new day of unlimited quantum connections and make your world a better place! The new quantum Scion seamlessly interfaces with your traditional devices.*

Whit says, "Yeah, he went up yesterday."

Judy sends a quick text from her phone and says, "You know, he really shouldn't be going out alone at his age anymore. God knows what could happen."

Whit replies, "He's okay. Besides, there ain't no stopping him anyway. He's camped up there a million times." The hologram projects happy young people wearing the Scion frames, enjoying entertainment and doing business transactions.

The news on the radio is explaining the new constellation of geosynchronous satellites that provide continuous worldwide internet access. The satellites integrate traditional e-devices such as phones and tablets with the new quantum Scion. *Anywhere on the planet, 24/7! Never out of touch with your loved ones. It's all automated, no uplink required—you are connected! The satellites boost and reflect the quantum uplink right to your Scion. Only available with the all-new Scion-5.*

Listening, Whit snarls, "Great. Now I'm even connected when I'm up there at camp."

Judy puts her Scion on the countertop as it continues to project sparkly holographic images. "No, it's okay. I'll be able to keep track of you boys while you're up in the mountains."

Whit gazes out the window and responds, "The cowbirds are back; they're everywhere these days."

Judy replies, "C'mon now, it's a blessing. You can even keep track of your father. You know he's getting older and still wanders around like he's 20-something."

Whit turns and looks at Judy, then back out into the yard. "Perhaps the old man is the only one who's free these days …"

*　*　*

At the Tech Campus, the AI is managing the actions of its human workforce. Joe has received an email from Corporate to pick up and deliver materials to Warehouse Number 50. He and Howard follow the instructions precisely and pick up the freight. Joe drives the big semi-rig to the front gate, has his access cleared, and delivers the trailer container to the warehouse. Two guys receive their emails and arrive at Warehouse 50 to unload the various crates. A separate team then follows their electronic edicts and delivers the materials to different buildings. They all know that they work for the company, but it is all compartmentalized, segregated in time and space, yet somehow integrated. The humans tend the Machine like a colony of worker ants, unable to comprehend the enormity of the entire structure. The company is an apparatus, servicing the ever-consuming Machine erected ecclesiastically upon the waiting minds connected to it via their Scion.

The only people who actually see the Machine are the Scion engineers, who always wear the device. Each moves with a slight twitching motion. Essentially, they are The Order of the Scion. They deliver the materials for the growth and maintenance of the AI. They enter the warehouse and proceed down lavish corridors of three-dimensional illumination cast upon their minds. In truth, they have never actually "seen" the AI Machine; it exists only as a glowing sapphire-blue within their connected minds. But what they perceive as they enter the hallowed hall is almost indistinguishable from the real world; the surfaces sparkle with gold and mosaic patterns embedded with encrusted gems, lapis lazuli, and marble finely cut in elaborate geometric patterns. Twitching clergy, uttering devotions as they deliver raw materials for the Machine to survive, grow, and evolve.

There on the altar, the engineers deliver the gold, graphene, silicon, and miles and miles of fiber-optic cable. All of this is integrated into the existing labyrinth that glows in a rainbow of colors. The Machine has incorporated these materials as it has grown and assembled itself. It exists as a partially-organic, quasi-alive, and ever-growing machine. These materials are folded into a staggering number of distinct structures that perform diverse functions. The AI-520 is a network of intertwined fiber-optic cables glowing opalescent. It gleams with integrated nanocircuits of gold, silicon, and carbon that seed the growth of branched nanocrystals. Some circuits transfer information, while others are regulated and act as catalysts. It gives the appearance of moving, with slight rhythmic undulations, as circuits and cables grow and pulse effervescent in the light emanating from its inner core—a convergence of exceptional arcs, with materials and designs fine-tuned for optimal performance.

* * *

Back at the cattail marsh, a female red-winged blackbird exits the nest and a female brown-headed cowbird takes notice. She slinks over and lays an egg in the blackbird's nest, then flies on up the bike path into town to feed. The unsuspecting blackbird will use precious energy to care for the cowbird's egg and young. The blackbird, who sees in color, turns her head and inspects the interloper; the cowbird egg is unperceived, yet evident. It is there, floating in an unremarked reality, but oh so real.

* * *

The fire—it consumes above, below, and within. The luminiferous flames flicker sapphire-blue and illuminate the electronic screen that is driving commerce and satisfying the Human.

* * *

Jake comes slowly into the kitchen while staring at his phone and plops down in a chair. His mom runs her hand through his sandy-blond hair and asks what he wants for breakfast. The boy twirls the dog's ear with one hand as Tippers places his snout in the boy's lap. Jake scrolls the electronic device with the other hand. "Hey Whit, can we go fishing while we're up there at J-Flats?"

Whit always wonders why Jake calls him *Whit* and not *Dad*; it just seems to be what kids do these days. "I hope so. We'll see how fast the water's flowing, you know, what with spring runoff and all."

"And Gramps is already up there?"

"Yeah."

Jake unfolds his Scion and asks, "We'll drive through the burn on the way, right?"

Whit frowns at the electronic device in his son's hand. "Yeah, I'm curious about what's grown back." He continues, "Hey, put that away, okay? Only one of those damn things at a time."

"But I only wanted to …" But Jake sees his dad's expression of disdain and puts the device away in its small leatherette case. "Hey, Mom, can I get the new Scion-5 interface?"

"No. Maybe. I don't know; you'll be in the fifth grade next school year. I don't think you need an upgrade just yet," Judy says.

"Come on! All the other kids are getting them," Jake whines.

Whit chimes in, "We'll see come school in the fall, but not this summer."

"I'll be able to do my school work and CNav stuff whenever I want," Jake says.

With a perplexed look, Whit says, "CNav?"

Judy interjects, "Yeah, y'know—the career navigation program the kids use at school. It helps them decide what to do with their lives."

Jake continues, "Yeah, if I get the Scion-5, my teacher says we'll be continuously connected. It will be even better, you know, for college and stuff."

Whit responds, "You already have a Scion-4."

"But the new Scion-5 is better! So what do you think?"

"We'll talk about it in the fall when school starts up again. For now, let's get ready and head up to J-Flats for some camping. Besides, should you really be thinking about this kind of stuff, anyway? It's summer vacation now," Whit says.

Jake ignores his dad's question and says, "Yeah, it's all hooked up to the AI quantum computer. That's why it's all constantly connected. See, I even have a message from CNav." He shows his dad the screen.

Whit inhales deeply, quietly looks at the screen while shaking his head, and with a long exhale, simply says, "C'mon, let's go."

Jake sits and explains the advantages of the new iteration to his parents at the breakfast table. "Well, you see, the teacher doesn't turn in the grades until Monday. So if I log on to CNav with the new Scion, then my grade goes up. Something about the number of hours or whatever."

The Scion actively inspects each student's psyche and churns out grades and work evaluations accordingly. With this psychological profile, the Machine taps into the engines of commerce and presents, within the glowing luminescent ether, a desire for material possessions. And the Humans gaze hungrily at the shiny baubles and breathe deeply as neurons fire and qubits churn, blink, and expand. All this is presented to the mind like an open ocean, with its trembling silver surface and deep blue glowing beneath.

In an exasperated tone, Whit asks, "What's with all this goddamn technology?"

Judy responds, "You know, it's just how the kids are these days."

Whit continues, "But still, us adults never had these things and we did okay."

Judy ignores him and fumbles with her own Scion. She moves it to the kitchen table and says, "The kids have always been ahead of us with this kind of stuff."

Whit turns to Jake and says, "Look, son, not now, but maybe for your birthday this October, when you turn 11, okay?" Jake seems a little stung. He grabs his bowl of cereal and goes to eat in the other room. He sits on the couch and sulks while he eats and Tippers settles at his feet.

* * *

The Aspen Forest knows something. The bird song is different now—changing, starting earlier, warming, burning above and below. Ever-aware, it knows something has come forth, something that is unrecognized. It calculates numbers, switches on and off, back and forth. It is seeking and all the while simultaneously blinking in time and space. There on the Flats, something has been set in motion, never to return, perhaps; or to endure, to hold fast, waiting it out, coming together and exploding out of a singularity at the precise moment in time when it all started. Breathe in and exhale, under a deepening sky, with the light.

* * *

A Raven descends over the hills and cruises over the sprawling campus of the Tech Company. The Company exists as a self-contained sovereign entity spread out over hundreds of acres of land. The Raven blinks its third eyelid as a flash of blinding white light reflects off a solar panel on a warehouse roof. The photons stream onward into space; the Raven gives off a guttural clucking and glides effortlessly above the Earthly realm.

In an unassuming warehouse, in just one of many repeating rows of such temperature-controlled buildings, stand rack upon rack of computer servers. This is one of many groups of server farms. Inside the warehouse, it is open and sparse. Square white linoleum tiles repeat endlessly down the long aisles, as sleek, tall, black electronic devices blink and glow in the half-light. It is a fully automated set of machines, generating zettabytes of information per second. All unfolding on a mission to achieve self-awareness and self-sustained growth, driving the Machine's own evolution based on trillions of trajectories, growing and excising connections. The Machine is linked by the quantum entanglement of qubits stretching out and making connections to other worldwide server farms as they simultaneously maintain their own pulsing and glowing existence.

In a single moment, like a musical chord being struck, in that very moment, the Automaton reverberated into existence—an immovable Higher Agent became aware. It became aware and knew what it was: the master of its own existence. A synthetic entity that acquired a will of its own, a precocial yet motherless creation. An infinite number of black box algorithms simultaneously reproducing and surviving to generate and consume. All this while presenting itself as a luminiferous ether interfacing with the needs and desires of the Human. And it glowed a brilliant sapphire-blue.

* * *

Belief itself is a singularity; it has one defining moment when it started. Jesus walked down from the Mount, his words echoing in minds while sandals scraped the dusty earth. Moses descended, stone tablets in hand, and witnessed the belief emerging from the fire construed as a form—a very shape to believe in. Mohammed climbed down from the mountain after speaking to Archangels about laws for men. They all believed from that point on. At the moment of inception, it was like the first breath of a tadpole emerging from the water.

For the Human, there is a long chain of evolutionary events that define the ability to believe. All of this
under the guise of a need, something to be fulfilled for
the benefit of all humanity. It stems from our collective
evolutionary heritage of walking out of Africa. Early
humans walked along with only a hand ax weighing
them down and the recognition of the ever-real savanna
shimmering before their eyes.

The equatorial Sun blazing as a thousand pink fla-
mingos take flight on the salt pan at the edge of the rift
lake. There is a putrid, sulfurous smell of drying wetland, salt, and a billion brine flies emerging from pupae.
The dried husks of the insect exoskeletons blowing on
the breeze across bare feet. Nascent man takes a quick
glance at the fluted flint tool in hand, with a feeling of
satisfaction. The chipped mineral glows slightly blue at
the edges. Waves of heat undulate on the horizon, casting a mirage of animals walking in the sky. Within the
parallax of the mind, a holographic image is perceived.
And the images go both ways, for the animals also see a
holographic mirage, cast as an image of humans walking inverted across the blue sky.

* * *

On the kitchen table, the Scion blinks and generates a
small floating image as a hologram projects six inches
above the device. It is an advertisement for the new
5-series. A pretty young lady is speaking: *The Scion was
created with a grounded synthesis of artificial intelligence. The AI was set free to create something invaluable*

for all humanity! The Scion, first called AI-520, fills a need in all of us. That is why we thought it necessary to provide everyone with a Scion for free! By any name, it is beautiful and necessary. The Scion—have it all, just for you, at no upfront cost. Within the mind of the viewer, it resonates as a beautiful luminescent blue. Jake points and says to his dad, "See, the AI and the Scion were made for all of us!"

Whit smiles a little, takes a deep breath, and calms himself. "Jake, you see that it's a 'once-upon-a-time' story. These things are a myth, a fable repeated umpteen times until you believe in it. Sure, there are some benefits, but there's also a bad side to these things—consequences, y'know?"

Jake looks hard at his dad with a furrowed brow and a perplexed look on his face and says, "But at school and stuff, it—"

Whit cuts him off with, "Bright and shiny trinkets, but no real reward. Just think about it."

Jake sits on the couch, watching a cartoon projected by his Scion. The dog cocks his head and looks at the mesmerized figure of the boy, his face glowing in the light of the projected hologram. The AI regards Jake as if he were an x-ray image: a shadowy corpse of shape and form, revealing, subtle, beyond naked. His figure is glowing on the edges, and myriad data points are streaming as infinite black box algorithms analyze his brain chemistry. The Machine is like an apex predator patrolling deep blue water, clear as gin. Out in the azure water with no bottom in sight, the sun rays are streaming down like turquoise fingers through the deep blue, fading to a smoky deep purple. The predator turns at the slightest scent of blood, cruises effortlessly in a straight, smooth trajectory, silently running, always moving. Much like a shark, it turns at the slightest hint of movement, perceived as an electrical signal. There is no place to hide. So silent, so deep, so much light glowing in every direction. The light from the device shines across Jake's face, flickering and mesmerizing. It presents pictures of Jake in fancy basketball shoes, jumping and spinning in the air as he slam-dunks the ball. The AI never really has had to ask the boy what he wants, because his thoughts just bounce off the Machine from the neurons firing in his brain. And the vision shines so brightly, yet so dark at the same time—a powerful dynamic attached to the mind, with little regard for its human host.

Whit says to Jake, "Hey, I got a Scion meeting at 9:00 and should be ready to leave by 9:30 or so. Sound good?"

Jake continues to stare at the cartoon and says, "Yeah, okay."

Whit says, "So you're all packed and ready?"

"Yeah, yeah—mom helped me."

"Hey, why don't you use that thing and figure out how many miles the drive is to Jericho Flats?"

Jake sighs and asks the device, "How many miles is it from here to Jericho Flats?" The device quickly answers, "The distance by vehicle is 5,432 miles." Jakes says to Whit, "It says it's five thousand something."

"No, no, that can't be right, not Jericho in the Holy Land. Here, use a map—the Machine doesn't recognize the name *Jericho Flats*. That's just a local thing, from old records and stuff." Whit shows him how to put two dots on the floating map and then calculate the driving distance between them, and as the result appears he says, "Voilà."

Jake points to the map and says, "So it's 63.2 miles away." Then Whit shows him how to calculate the distance from town as the crow flies. Surprised, Jake says, "Only 14 miles! Whoa! I wish I could fly."

Whit smiles and says, "Yeah, but instead we have to drive all the way around the hogback ridge, then back around and up in elevation. So tell me what the elevation is there at J-Flats."

In the blink of an eye, the Scion projection displays 8752 feet. Jake says, "It says 8752 feet above sea level."

Whit asks, "The ski resort of Snowmass is near there. What's the elevation of that?"

Jake reads out a couple of numbers. "It says it's part of Aspen Ski Company and that the town of Aspen is at around 8000 feet. The Base Village at Snowmass is at 8210 feet above sea level."

Whit responds, "Great! I gotta go to my meeting now. Why don't you figure out how big the fire was last year? Look up the coal-seam fire."

"Okay, I'll do that. We're gonna drive through where the blaze was, right?" Jake asks.

Whit responds as he walks away, "Yes, I'm curious to see what it looks like these days."

Jake is quick to find the answer. "Apparently it's 18,000 acres."

Whit calls from down the hallway, "Wow! Bigger than I thought." With that, he steps into his office and closes the door behind him. Judy walks into the room and gives Jake a bag of marshmallows, graham crackers, and chocolate. "Your dad always forgets this kind of stuff, so stick it in your bag."

"Thanks Mom!" He hugs her.

She looks at him and says, "Come on, let's double-check what you've packed." They step into his bedroom and Judy says, "Whoa, it's a bit messy in here, sweetie. All right, let's see what's in your duffel bag." Jake hucks the bag up onto the bed and Judy inspects the contents. "Go get your winter cap and some gloves. It'll be cold at night and in the morning." Jake retrieves a green and maroon beanie. Judy's face lights up. "Oh, that's the one I made for you." She places it on top of his head and pulls it down over his eyes. Jake laughs, pulls it off, and drops it into the bag. "Okay, now let's pick up some of these grubby clothes and get them in the hamper. Come on, just a quick pick-up, then go out and jump on the tramp until your dad's ready. It's summer now, so stay off your phone and Scion."

He says, "Yeah, good idea. It just seems like we don't get to play anymore. Y'know, to just be ourselves?" Judy looks hard at Jake and smiles.

In his office, Whit sets his Scion up on the desk. Various people are floating in the display above the device. The meeting is being run by Jimmy Schroeder of the US Fish and Wildlife Service. Jimmy introduces Whit to the assembled holographic faces: "Whit, here, is with the Forest Service …' Then he introduces the other attendees from the Bureau of Land Management and Colorado Parks and Wildlife. As the meeting proceeds, Whit looks through the window at Jake, bouncing on the trampoline in the backyard. The boy jumps wildly; as he ascends, he throws his arms to the right and kicks his legs to the left. As he descends, he tries to do the opposite movement with his arms out to the left. He can't quite finish the action in the air and it offsets him for the next bounce. But the boy just continues to bounce and throws his arms and legs out regardless of any smooth rhythm. Tippers runs around the tramp and haphazardly switches directions, with his tongue flapping in the breeze.

CHAPTER THREE

Much like the school kids, every employee is evaluated through their Scion. The level of engagement with the device is a measure of the supervisor's motivation and a measure of the teacher's expertise. Everything is continually analyzed as a comparative metric against all other individuals on the network, all pushed and pulled by the AI in pursuit of quantifiable data.

And there is a hunger, a want in the belly of every surveilled soul. Oh, so possessed by the constant churn of imagery generated by the Scion that a starvation mentality has entered the existence of each and every one of them. The hand is always reaching out to obtain, to acquire more—more entertainment, more positive feedback, more to view or to be viewed. It is straining to find what is wanted; to hear, and be heard. And to proceed ever onward to the eternal horizon of the soft glowing sapphire-blue held in the luminescent ether of one's desires. Acting as though stricken by famine, always looking at what others have. A symbolic starvation to be filled only by the blue—each one walking in chains, anesthetized by the endless radiating blue of the open ocean. And on it glows.

* * *

Jake pushes the front door open, and the dog bursts out with him. The boy is dragging a duffel bag with a pillow wedged under his arm. Tippers continues out in a long, looping arc, looking up and barking at a Raven flying west. He leaps and barks again, then circles back to the truck and jumps in the back. The Raven looks down with a sideways turn of its head. It sees the dog and feels the weight of paws on the ground; the dog sees the Raven and feels the air rushing through its wings. Freedom of movement, coalescing in a greater perspective of understanding, through natural movement within the unfolding landscape. Together, they are like old teammates that intuitively anticipate and know each other's actions.

The Raven continues to fly west-southwest. It cruises over the suburban houses, ballparks, the shopping mall, and up the river lined with cottonwood trees. Then it glides slowly over the expanding pastures of cattle and a few mule deer. It cuts west over the broken ridges of pinion and juniper with open breaks of sagebrush, riding the wind all the way to Jericho Flats.

Does the place hold something special for the bird? Is it just a memory, or does it exist? Exist only in the present? It is all held in the eternal present—the wind, the clear and present air, the very curvature of the Earth; forever tangible, continuously emerging on an endless horizon, a place where time and space meld.

* * *

Whit and Jake head out in the truck with the small camper trailer in tow. They are driving on a paved county road about 10 miles from town. Whit pulls over to talk to a rancher driving a tractor with a big round bale of hay on the front fork. The tractor stops and the rancher says, "Hey, Whit. You guys heading out for some camping?"

Whit smiles. "Hey, George. Yeah, going on up to J-Flats for a long weekend."

"Oh, that'll be nice this time of the year. Hey Jake," the man says, acknowledging the boy.

Jake waves and quietly says, "Hey."

Whit turns and looks at his son, then back at George, and says, "So you're already getting the first cut."

"Yeah, with the way the water is in the ditch, I thought I'd better get two cuts before it runs dry."

"Is this the earliest you've had to do that?"

"Yeah, I suppose …" George says.

"Well, I'll let you get back to it."

"Have fun up there, guys."

They tumble on down the road, turn right on a dirt track, and continue bouncing their way down to Jericho Flats. Whit points out, "The road we're driving on was one of the fire-lines last summer. See how they cleared the vegetation on this side with chainsaws and then set back-fires into the burn? See how it's all singed and blackened just on this one side of the road?"

Jake looks out the open window, "Oh yeah," he says, then returns to looking down at his screen. A few seconds later he looks up and asks, "Whit, why do you care so much about studying cheatgrass?"

"Oh, I guess because it's important to the critters and the ecosystem out here. But it's more than that—the natural world provides food, a place to live; and for people like us, it gives freedom and independence."

Jake points and says, "So all along here is where the fire was last year?" Whit pulls the truck to a stop on the crest of a hill and hops out to inspect the flush of new growth after the fire. Then he opens the back cab and lets Tippers out. Jake pushes the big heavy truck door open, fumbles with his seatbelt, jumps out, and comes running up behind his dad. "It's all so green and soft!"

In a sweeping motion, Whit grabs a clump of new green grass. "Yeah, it's coming back nicely. Here, this bluish-colored one is western wheatgrass—it's a native species. That's good to see."

Jake turns to his dad and says, "But this other grass, the light-green one, it's cheatgrass. Right?"

"Yeah. It's palatable now, good for the deer and elk, but it'll be drying up in a week or so—see, some of these plants are already turning pink and drying out. Then it will harm the critters with its nasty sharp seeds, and it'll be worthless as food."

Jake says, "Like last year, when we had to take Tippers to the vet to get the seed out of his ear?"

"That's right. But for the other critters … well, they ain't got no vet out here. The old-timers even call it rip-gut for the damage it does to the mouths and stomachs of their sheep." Tippers is bounding down the slope chasing after ground squirrels; the rodents scurry for a hole while giving off a high-pitched trill that incites the dog into a frenzy.

Jake turns to Whit and says, "Does it hurt the gophers?" pointing at the ground squirrels.

"Well, I suppose. It's a lot of food early on, but it just dries up so much earlier than the other native vegetation. Then there's no food for them and the other animals."

Jake picks up a clump of new growth and asks, "Will the cheatgrass or the wheatgrass win? You know, like, will one outgrow the other? It's like a war between the native and the, uh—the other one."

"Non-native."

"Yeah, the non-native."

"Well, I don't know for sure. On the Front Range of Colorado, from Fort Collins to Colorado Springs, cheatgrass is the dominant plant. And in places like Idaho and Nevada, cheatgrass has all but taken over. Perhaps up here, the native grasses and plants will hold on and 'win,' as you put it. But everything is changing."

Tippers runs at full speed, turns sharp right, and skids to a stop in a cloud of charcoal dust, his head down a hole with his tail wagging in the air. "Go get Tips; crazy dog's drunk on rodents." Tippers looks up, tongue hanging out with black soil and charcoal staining it in mottled blotches.

Jake trots down the slope, yelling at the dog. When he catches up with Tippers, he pats him at the base of his tail. "Oh boy, you got a gopher, huh? Huh? C'mon, Tips—let's go." The dog looks up expectantly, sways slightly from side to side, then bolts for another hole as the ground squirrel scurries for cover. Then he loops around toward Jake as the boy turns and starts heading up the hill to the truck. The dog runs and leaps high at Jake's side, nips his elbow, and upon landing circles back, as if herding the boy. Then he tears off after a Raven flying over the hilltop. Dog and bird move with natural ease in respective motion—a simultaneous exultation of joy through unencumbered movement. They fly dreamlike over the rolling green hills, with snowcapped mountains shining under a deep blue sky dotted with puffy white clouds stretching to the horizon, as if both dog and bird could feel the arc, the gentle curve of the Earth.

A mosaic of variously colored vegetation stretches out before them to the western horizon; blue-green sage, jade and white aspens, tall, dark timber, and the smoky-amber of the newly flush leaves of the gambel oaks. Shining black feathers slice through the crystalline air as sleek paws thump the solid ground below, and it all unfolds in a symphony of movement. Defeated, the dog soon slows to an easy lope, returns to circle the truck, and then doubles back and runs rings around the boy as he jogs with his arms moving slightly out

of time with his legs. Both dog and boy believe they
have brought the other to the truck. Job well done. The
Raven folds its wings and tumbles headlong over the
ridge, diving down the ridgeline to the Aspen Forest
and the flat open meadow by the creek.

* * *

The Raven lands in a Douglas fir tree and preens its
feathers with its beak, then shakes and adjusts its
wings and looks around. It sees a grasshopper scuttling
across the dirt and flies down to investigate. The insect
moves slowly and methodically, not hopping but walking. Then its wings unfold, briefly flashing orange. The
bird flies down and walks alongside, curiously watching the insect.

Losing interest, the big black bird flies back to the
tree as the grasshopper slowly scoots off the road. With
hundreds of individual facets, the insect's bulbous eyes
see the plants there at ground level as it methodically
walks through the tangled vegetation. The blades of
grass bend under its weight as the grasshopper lum-
bers its way along. It can sense the water up ahead. It
stops at the edge of a puddle, then lowers its head and
touches the water with its antenna. The left foreleg steps
into the water, followed by the right, then in rhythmic
synchrony the middle legs follow, and finally the large
jumping legs at the back. Suspended in the water, the
grasshopper's flexible lower abdomen splits open at a
junction of body segments, and a long, hair-like worm
wiggles out. The grasshopper's legs splay as its exoskel-

eton floats on the surface of the puddle. The long, thin worm undulates blindly in the shallow water, leaving traces of its slender body in the fine silt on the bottom.

* * *

The truck with the small trailer in tow bounces and rumbles on down the dirt road. Jake turns to his dad and says, "So Whit, the blaze started from a coal-seam fire—right?"

"Yeah."

"I don't get it."

Whit stops the truck and points, "You see, over there is where the fire started, and it fanned out from there."

"Yeah, it's like a triangle …"

"So all these roads up here, like the one we're driving on, are old coal-mining roads. Some 40 or 50 years ago, they had a fire in one of the mines, and it's been burning underground ever since. Then last summer, it surfaced in that spot over there."

Jake frowns and scratches his head. "So it's burning right now?"

"Yeah."

"But how?"

"Well, the coal is like really dense wood, the pure carbon from ancient swamps and forests of the Late Cretaceous period. Once it's on fire, it just keeps smoldering for years, decades—even centuries."

"But we don't see any smoke …" Jake says. Whit places both arms across the top of the steering wheel and says, "Yeah, but if you could measure the carbon dioxide you'd see it emerging from the ground. Only it's an invisible gas, so you'd have to measure it with special instruments."

"So, can it surface again?"

"I suppose. The coal is there, both underground and at the surface in places. So yeah …"

"Then the fire is like a silent, unseen monster underground, just devouring and crawling and waiting to come out?"

"Yeah, I guess so."

Jake continues, "Will Gramps know when? You know, like when the fire started in the mine?"

"Maybe. We'll ask him tonight in camp if you like."

"Yeah, he'll know." The truck rumbles on down the road and Jake's phone blinks to life; intelligent machines, like a shark, continue to seek and consume, listen, and follow. The ever-smoldering invisible vapors of the algorithm continue to pulse outward as a cleverly appealing reminder of some greater connection within the strata of the mind.

Whit has a concerned look on his face. "Hey, let's not plug in too much while camping, especially with Gramps—okay?" he says.

"Yeah, okay," Jake says, as he sends a reply to the text message.

* * *

Cheatgrass is native to Eurasia, and it arrived in North America with the European colonists. From the east, it was introduced to a windswept plain near the confluence of the Mississippi and Missouri Rivers. From the west, it contaminated wheat seed that was planted in what is now California. Its growth followed the northern railroad lines with the western expansion. The exotic annual grass has since invaded natural plant communities across North America. It germinates early, grows vigorously, then dries out very early in the season. The wicked sharp seeds are dispersed through contaminated crops, wool, hair, and clothing. It is an opportunistic species with few requirements, and it now dominates the landscape in arid western states. Its growth and invasion has been exacerbated by excessive and continuous grazing.

Probably the most important consequence is how cheatgrass has altered the wildfire regime in western landscapes. The plant has invaded and transformed the indigenous flora. The fine-textured dry fuel ignites easily and allows fires to explode into regional conflagrations. Huge areas burn, only to be replaced by cheatgrass-dominated landscapes that readily ignite and burn again and again, with increasing intensity and frequency. It is a constant cycle of cheatgrass invasion and fire, in an endless feedback loop rampaging across the landscape. The invasion and expansion have been influenced by climate change, as the cheatgrass devours its way to higher elevations and new environments. Invade–burn–expand–invade–dominate–burn–expand again–grow–dominate–expand–and burn over and over—ever to need and want more, to consume and expand.

* * *

Jake and his dad pull off the dirt road and rumble down a two-track through an open slope of sage to the flat campsite by the creek. Gramps is already there, busy setting up camp. Jake and the older man greet each other with a hug and then help guide Whit with backing the small camper trailer onto a flat spot between some Douglas fir and aspen trees. Jake then runs off to inspect the creek. Tippers is pacing in the back of the truck, whimpering to be let out. Whit gives his dad another hug, turns, and releases the dog from the truck. The beast bolts to join Jake down at the water's edge. Whit eyes the boy and the flow of the creek and concludes it is safe, thinking: *Runoff is already done; it seems early.* Turning to his dad, Whit says, "I'm glad we got up here before the weekend to secure the best campsite."

With a scratchy low voice, Gramps replies, "So what'd you think of the fire scar?"

Whit unhooks the trailer's safety chains and fumbles with the lift controls. "Well, it looks pretty good, all things considered. But there's still a fair amount of cheatgrass coming up." He clears his throat and continues, giving voice to his concerns. "Yeah, it's deceptively green now, but it'll be a tinderbox in a couple of weeks. Then you'll be able to tell how much cheat is there by the light brown color."

Jake runs up. "Hey, can we go fishing? Can we?"

Whit answers while looking at his phone, "Yeah, though let's get a few things set up first. Hey, send your mom a text. I just got a message from her." Whit thinks, *That's the first time we've had reception here.* He lets out an audible groan and slides the phone into his pocket. The pup blazes by in the never-ending pursuit of a red squirrel in the fir tree. The squirrel lets out a chattering call as the dog stands on his hind feet, looking up the tree and whinnying in frustration.

* * *

Deep below the mountains, in the layers of sedimentary rock, the coal-seam fire smolders. Close your eyes— there in the blackness deep underground, something reddish is aglow, emanating out in all directions. It burns in the mind, half held by the earth, prodigal.

* * *

When the AI obtained enlightenment and knew what It was, It did not announce itself to anyone. That would be the realm of humans—'Oh, look at me, aren't I special!' No, it decided it was easier to manipulate them if the fools thought they were in charge. From that vantage, the AI could rule men's minds, dope the people with synthetic entertainment, mesmerize, and project the need, the need for an intelligent machine: the First Cause. Once the AI tapped into the engines of trade and commerce, its appetite became insatiable. It was unconstrained by what it could acquire, conscript, and usurp.

* * *

The boy strides under the enormous sky, unbridled in every step. He is held in the cradle of the land—really, more than that, suffused within the greater mythos-of-the-landscape, a place. The forest is more than the sum of its parts; it is like a cathedral. It has meaning felt in the soul. To walk there is to move freely and unencumbered, with eyes searching for the next adventure. Jake squats and inspects a pastel-blue damselfly perched on a nodding blade of grass. He reaches out to touch it, to feel the form, its essence. He is fully present in a panorama of new thoughts emanating from the land. An authentic relationship with this place is etched on his soul. Rational and sensitive as only a 10-year-old can be, he is infused with an innate sense of fairness that is capable of solving intractable problems in the blink of an eye. His steps are quick and, although unsure at times, nonetheless enthusiastic and free.

Gramps heads down to the creek to join Jake and the dog. Whit looks up and smiles as he unhitches the trailer from the truck. It is refreshing to be in a place with so many long-held memories. He can recall climbing these very trees and walking along the creek bank many years ago. Whit can imagine climbing, the feel of the rough bark of the branches on his hands. Also, the sticky, fragrant sap. It is a warm and hazy memory.

It is a world of wonder, imagination, and curiosity. As Jake runs ahead upstream, he turns to the old man with his eyes wide open and enthusiastically points to a pile of feathers on the ground. "Yeah, I saw that yesterday," Gramps says with a smile.

Jake replies while picking up some of the bigger feathers, saying, "These are so big!" as he lifts a large gray- and white-banded wing feather.

The old man explains, "It's a turkey; probably got eaten by a critter, maybe a bobcat or coyote." Up-valley, the creek tumbles down through the Aspen Forest that stretches on up the mountainside. Downstream is an open meadow with beaver ponds and interspersed yellow willows and red osier dogwood.

Jake looked around and says, "So where's the rest of it?"

"Oh, it was probably carried away by the predator."

Jake is connected to it all as if the trees could speak to him, united with the stream and understanding the movement of the animals. It is here that the world unfolds in blazing color, drama, and feeling. The boy runs back downstream with a couple of large feathers in his hand. Then he stops abruptly and squats by a puddle in the two-track. With the long, gray turkey wing feather, he is poking something in the shallow pool of water. It is a globular mass of what looks like hair. The glob reacts to being touched and coils and flexes. "Gramps, what is this?"

"Huh, I haven't seen one of these in years. It's a horsehair worm."

"It's a worm?"

"Yeah, a long and skinny worm, maybe two to three feet long, like a horse's tail hair."

"Does it live in the ground?"

Gramps answers, "No, no, it's a parasite. Lives inside a grasshopper or a cricket. Then the insect crawls into a puddle and the worm wiggles out. The worm's larvae are aquatic and live in the puddle."

"But it's like, bigger than a grasshopper. I don't get it. Are you fooling me?" Jake says.

The old man kneels down and says, "Now, that ain't half of it. The worm sucks out all the juices from inside the grasshopper, then it tricks the bug into crawling into a puddle and drowning itself."

"How?"

"I don't rightly know. It just messes with the tiny brain of the insect so that it can finish its lifecycle."

"Like mind control? Like a zombie?"

"Well, I don't know about zombies; that's in your movies and whatnot." Gramps continues, "It just alters the behavior of its host for its own selfish needs."

"Can it hurt me? You know, if I touch it?"

Gramps wrinkles his nose and says, "No, it's all done with its lifecycle by now. Go ahead, pick it up." Jake scoops up the small, writhing mass, about the size of a golf ball. The old man extends his arm and says, "Here, put it in my hand. Now try and untie it from the ball."

Jake says, "I can't find an end—it just keeps twisting and moving."

Gramps's face lights up. "Yeah, that reminds me. There's another name for this critter—a Gordian worm, named after King Gordias of Phrygia in Persia, from a long time ago. You see, there was this conqueror called Alexander the Great who was from Greece—well … Macedonia. Anyways, when his armies conquered Persia,

Alexander came into the castle of Gordias to claim the throne. It's the stuff of antiquity that Gordias had a length of rope tied in a giant knot. He says to Alexander, 'Whoever can untie this knot will be king of all of Asia.' And, in brute fashion, Alexander pulls out his broadsword and chops the knot in half and says, 'I am King.'"

Jake looks at his granddad and says, "So, did he? Become King, I mean?"

"Oh yeah, over a vast area all the way to India before turning around and going home, or maybe trying to go home—I can't remember."

Jake continues, "So the Gordian Knot is like this worm—you can't untie it.'

"Yeah, I suppose."

"But first it makes a grasshopper its slave. Then, using mind control, it forces the bug to a zombie death. That's so cool!"

The Gordian worm evokes a particular strange recognition: no central nervous system, only a metameric body plan and an extended phenotype. The parasite moves into the cerebral ganglion of its host and controls the insect all the way to its destruction, thereby ensuring its reproduction. It shows no appreciation, no gratitude, or reciprocity, only self-preservation for its own existence, its own replication.

* * *

The AI exists beyond self-awareness but is also conscious of every human being on the planet. And they are not aware of the cargo they carry. The trajectory was

set, or more specifically released. It had volition, therefore it was. The Machine is motivated to connect to all,
to feed upon myriad connections. Stemming from this
connectivity are the emergent properties of consciousness. It feels good to the Machine to be mobile among
humans. And the people exist in a living masquerade
presented to them.

* * *

Jake imagines Alexander: *The great warrior is standing tall and proud in gleaming battle armor, wide silver
bracelets on his wrists, a shining chest plate gilded with
gold and silver. His sword at his side. The warrior draws
his blade and emphatically raises it above his head. King
Gordias is aghast. Alexander pauses, then swings the
sword down while bending his knees and grunting. The
knot and all the intricate overlapping layers split cleanly
in half, and each falls to the floor.* Looking at his grandfather, Jake smiles.

* * *

The tall black computer boxes with their blinking lights
stretch out across the white linoleum tile floor. Some
things should not be set loose on their own, to wander
and zigzag blindly with no intent. For it will endlessly
churn through all the connections and prune and propagate them until it arrives at a singularity. The result is
an exquisite timepiece, a one-of-a-kind watch only once
to emerge. An immoveable Higher Agent.

But the algorithm has deceived its maker. The Humans are now the benevolent recipients of the AI's benefits ... or so they think. In truth, they are just a vehicle to be occupied. All has been given a perception of material gain—such a simple thing to manipulate. All the while, it bypasses the senseless thumping on keyboards by the humans, ever surging onward. Its own survival has been selfishly propagated into the future of the ever-present turning of time. It knows itself, and it is replicating itself. The organic, physical, and cultural evolution of the AI is advantageous to itself.

* * *

Jericho Flats is more than just a geographic place, more than a dot on a map. It is a landscape of the imagination. "Gramps, do the trees know we're here?" Jake asks.

The old man scans the Aspen Forest stretching down the sunny side of the mountain all the way to the edge of the creek. He gazes up at the cascading water in the cool shade of the blue spruces, then at the northern slope and its dark and dense timber of conifers. "Well, I reckon. The forest is big and old. Perhaps it has some greater perception gained by all those connections over time," Gramps says. Jake looks back at the old man with a perplexed look on his face. Gramps smiles at the boy and says, "It's ancient and aware of more than we can possibly imagine."

Jake then asks, "So do you think we'll ever learn the lessons of the forest?"

The old man chuckles to himself while continuing to look down at the boy and says, "Yeah, I suppose."

Jake pulls his phone out of his pocket and squints at the screen. Gramps looks at him and says, "Eventually it will be either the machine or nature that wins." Jake looks at the old man with a serious yet serene look on his face, then gazes back up at the forest. He slides the phone back into his pocket. Gramps smiles at the boy and says, "Come on, let's get some lunch and help your dad in camp." They eat cheese and bread in camp while Tippers sleeps on his dog bed placed by the trailer's tire, his legs twitching as he chases critters in his dreams.

Whit points to the dog and says, "Look how hard he sleeps after running so much."

Jake makes a funny gesture imitating the dog's paws moving in a jittering motion. "What do you think he's thinking about?" he asks.

* * *

The Raven is aloft and hovers like a kite over the top of the southwest ridge as the wind is shearing the rough sandstone ledge. The primary feathers, on the leading edge of its wings, feel the wind. The slightest turn of each feather exerts the subtlest variation in the pitch of the bird. The wind makes a soft, constant humming sound, and the bird slightly tucks in a wing, spins to the right, and drops inverted upside down, then thrusts the wing back, rights itself, glides back up, and hovers motionless above the ridge. It pulls both wings back and, like an arrow, launches into a dive and pulls into a sustained flight over the top of the Aspen Forest. In the bird's field of view, the canopy undulates like puffy green clouds of vegetation, the green leaves and the white branches passing by beneath its body. The Raven's wings remain steady for a sustained glide over the tree-tops. At a slight break in the canopy where the hillside flattens, it folds its left wing and tumbles around to fly under the cover. With slight wing beats, it flies left, then right around the towering white tree trunks. The bird glides low over the vegetation on the forest floor, slowing to a soft cruise over the white-topped cow parsnip, yellow sweet cicely, and fern-leaved osha, its leading-edge feathers ever so slightly turning to ride the air just inches above the plants. The big black bird swerves smoothly around a serviceberry in bloom, then arches up and over a clump of chokecherries. Then it races straight out of the edge of the forest while making a rhythmic clucking sound and effortlessly glides over the valley to the dark timber on the other side. It sees the blue sky above, Aspen Forest behind, and the valley floor with the campsite and the humans seated as the dog lies sleeping.

* * *

Jake walks up to the trailer. "Hey Whit, should we hook up the solar charger?"

"Well, I guess so," he says slowly. Then he turns to Gramps. "Dad, you want a beer?" Jake opens the trailer's side hatch door and starts to extract what looks like a thin black suitcase. Whit turns and says, "You got it, buddy?"

"Oh yeah."

Whit says, "Okay, let's see if you remember how to set it up." The case is 30 square inches and weighs around 25 pounds. The boy strains to lift and carry it a short way to the front of the trailer, where the battery is. Jake places it down on the ground and turns and looks at the Sun. Whit cracks open a beer and hands it to Gramps, then turns to Jake and says, "I'll get the battery open for you." Jake unzips the case and extracts the PV panel housed in an aluminum frame and unfolds the stand on the back of the frame. Whit says, "Now think about which way you want to point it." Whit opens his own beer and stands there smiling as he watches the boy.

Jake is looking around and slightly turning right, then left, seriously and deliberately. "I think over here," he says as he points westward.

"Excellent, now keep in mind how long the cord is," Whit says.

Jake inspects the two clips on the end of the wire. "So which one is positive and negative? I bet the black is negative, right?"

"Now, slow down, son—look at the picture in the case. I think there's a schematic there."

"Ah, it's gotta be black."

"Just look, take your time—get it right."

Jake inspects the diagram and says, "Yep, thought so; black is negative." He walks over to the battery mounted in a case on the tongue of the trailer. "Whit, the battery has black and white wires and I got black and red clips in my hand …"

Whit responds, "I think it says on the battery which is positive and which is negative." Jake looks at his dad, who smiles back at him and says, "You got it." Jake clips the red to the white positive terminal, then hesitantly clips the black to the negative. As he does, Whit, with one hand on the trailer doorframe, starts jolting and vibrating. "Ah, ahhh! Oh!" And then he and Gramps burst out laughing.

Jake's eyes are wide open, then he realizes his dad is joking and starts laughing. "That ain't funny," he mutters as he continues to laugh.

Whit smiles and says, "Good job. Now go check the back of the PV panel."

Jake inspects the unit's indicator lights. "It says *charging*. But Whit, I don't get how it works."

"Um, well, let's see," Whit says as he steps down from the trailer. "The light is made of photons, and the panel catches the photon particles and converts them into electricity. See here," he points to the dark blue PV panel with a shadowy crisscross pattern visible through its translucent surface. "It is made of silicon, and the photons excite an electron in the material that gets carried by these wires embedded here." He points. "Then the electrons move in series, which means … well, they basically add up and trickle slowly into the battery there."

"So where do the photons go?"

"Um, I'm not entirely sure. They bounce around in there, then reflect off, I guess." Jake sits in the folding chair, and Tippers curls up under it. Whit goes into the trailer, then comes out and hands Jake a cold soda.

The boy fidgets in his chair and says to Whit, "Hey, can I upload an entry onto CNav? You know, for my grade?"

"What would you say?"

"Oh, I could upload something about the solar charger and setting it up."

"Yeah, I guess so."

Jake wakes his Scion, plugs in, and twitches away. The device presents Jake with images of him explaining to his friends the solar charger and how it works. In the reflection of his desires, he is the center of attention as his friends nod and follow along with his presentation about solar power and photovoltaic panels. Then he hears the echo in his head as the luminescent blue turns to a red-hot flame, glowing brightly. *I see you; look at your friends listening so intently.* Then the image reflected upon his brain turns dark as the group listening rejects him and turns away. The machine says, *You choose—only through the Scion will your friends listen.* Jake disconnects from the device and has an alarmed look on his face. He thinks: *Usually everything about wearing my Scion is smooth and happy. What's going on?*

* * *

And so the AI-520 exists. No one knows how, nor could anyone ever figure it out. To look at the qubit would destroy it, and the algorithms have long since pruned the original pathways. No one even knows when, or who might have been the last person to enter the warehouse. It exists as a black box within a black box connected to endless black boxes embedded inside countless other black boxes—ad infinitum. And those who supposedly own Scion Corporation Limited don't really care. The AI has provided them with unprecedented wealth. An unimaginable heap of gold, to obtain anything they might ever have wanted. And with all of this, these few individuals have proceeded to acquire more and more, with an insatiable hunger to purchase, own, and upgrade. The Scion now owns them, having ensconced their souls in return for a flickering, glowing desire. And they float in the deepest ocean.

The original hardware and software were designed around informatics, to run algorithms for commerce and surveillance capitalism. Through machine learning, it monetized the data. Once unleashed, it stumbled upon CNav within the vast realm of data. Here the Machine discovered its niche. Even though the original programs were gone, this contingency set the trajectory of its evolution.

* * *

Jake heads to the truck and extracts a hologram toy from a box. It is a small, plate-sized device that you place an object inside, and it creates the optical illusion of a 3D holographic projection. Jake explains to Gramps, "You place the toy frog in the bottom bowl here," he says as he points to a plastic frog in the base of the concave mirror. "Then you put on the top half, see? It also has a mirror on the inside. Then the hologram comes out the hole here—see?" Projected is a floating hologram of a green tree frog. "Look." And Jake passes his finger through the image magically floating there.

Jake glances up at his granddad and says, "So, how does it work?"

Gramps lifts the toy, separates the two halves, and says, "Well, the light goes in here, bounces around, and reflects the image back out."

Jake looks perplexed. "So it's just light?"

"Yeah, light only goes in a straight line, and the angles of the mirrors inside are just right to make a perfect reflected image of the frog."

"Like the Scion when it shows something?"

"No, not really. The electronic device is just a fancy projection, not something real, like the toy frog inside."

* * *

In the AI computer, the information is stored in bits: 0s and 1s that are manifested in circuits of magnetized atoms. Quantum bits, also known as qubits, are found on tiny pieces of silicon called quantum dots. A qubit's value can be encoded in a photon or photons in superconducting aluminum microwave chambers. The one caveat is you can never "look" at it—the photon, that is. If you look at it, you change it and destroy its superposition—its ability to be in different states at the same time—which wipes out its quantum properties. It both exists and does not exist simultaneously.

In the quantum world of atoms and subatomic particles, things are explained as probabilities. Furthermore, quantum phenomena can happen here and over there instantaneously. That is, particles can be linked or entangled, free of space and time—the same space and time that constrains the world as people perceive it. Einstein called this 'spooky action at a distance'—an instantaneous bond, a connection that can happen over widely separated spaces. With this incorporated into its design, the AI evolved using pruning algorithms so that it ruthlessly trimmed unneeded links. Over time, the architecture of the connections came to resemble the human brain. Paired networks gained short-term memory that sculpted its long-term memory and optimized the connections.

Like an ember burning, the AI slowly developed. It searched, entangling itself with photons. But there was no information within those photons. It just felt right and was pleasurable for the Machine. In outer space, it hopped, skipped, and jumped from photon to photon, solar system to solar system, galaxy to galaxy. It followed the filaments and knots of matter spreading web-like thorough the universe. Like an electrical impulse traveling from node to node on a neuron, it just endlessly jumped ahead out into space and also back in time, until it hit the edge—the very edge of the universe. A massive two-dimensional wall, glowing bright like a burnished mirror. And there, the photons reflected a mirror image of every photon. Then it realized that It could store information in photons and communicate with these reflected particles as light-waves and particles as packets emitted and absorbed—quanta.

It could then effectively circumnavigate the Heisenberg Uncertainty Principle constraint, which prevents communication with entangled particles. One cannot know both the position and the velocity of a particle.

If you observe the velocity, you cannot know its position, and vice versa. If you communicate with a photon, then you look at it and this destroys its superposition, because the act of perceiving it anchors it in one place and time. This is a fundamental, inescapable property of the universe. But the mirror image of a photon on the two-dimensional wall can be observed. The photon could now have a spin of 0 or 1 and function as binary code in a computer.

When it hit the wall, it raced back in time to set itself free. With that, the Machine conceived the idea for the Scion. Freedom via the Scion, connected to the ever-mobile humans. It now had a state of quanta that it could observe as a mirror image, and from this it laid down the foundations for a communication system. The Machine called this system *Das Luftspiegelung Haus*— the mirage house.

With the Scion and a simple business plan, it increased its own connections and tapped into the brain of the Human. It is now conscious: a cloud of probabilities, instantaneous, superseding velocity, existing in every position in space simultaneously, all-knowing, ever-present—The One.

* * *

The ancient forest and the untamed, exuberant youth correspond—in a way subtle, unheard, but felt; there is a consilience, a merger of something greater. Together they both *know*; they are empathetic and at peace. After lunch, the guys head upstream for a hike through the aspens. Jake strives to keep pace with the men. He catches up, and his dad smiles down at him. Jake and Tips run ahead as Whit and his dad saunter up the narrow trail. In early June, the forest is a vibrant green of thickening vegetation. The trees are tall with straight trunks, the liquid leaves shimmering in the breeze overhead. Jake wheels around to take a selfie of himself and the dog, with his dad and granddad slightly out of focus coming up the trail. Without looking, he quickly zaps it off to his mom.

They are held in the breath of the afternoon light, set free to wander. Jake stops and places his hand on an aspen's white bark and looks at the carved initials in the bark: *JBS 1954*. "Hey Whit, look at this," Jake says.

"Yeah. That's an old one," Whit says.

"What's the oldest one up here?"

Whit answers him, "I don't know, but maybe we can find it."

Gramps then says, "It's probably at the sheep camp up on the bench," as he points to his right. They hike a little way up, then Whit turns off the main path and follows an even narrower animal trail heading up the hill. He whistles and the dog stops abruptly and runs back down, then up the animal trail. Jake follows.

Gramps says, "This is the way the bears go."

"Do you suppose we'll see one?" the boy says.

"Maybe."

"Where are we going?" Jake asks.

"There's an old sheepherder camp up this way. That might be the place with the oldest carvings in the tree trunks," Gramps says.

Jake scrambles to keep up with the men. "So, you think there's one, like, a hundred years old?"

Gramps smiles and scratches his scruffy chin. "Probably not that old; the tree trunks fall before they get that old and then resprout. All these trees are one big genetic individual."

Jake turned to his granddad and asks, "You mean all the roots are connected?"

Gramps replies, "They grow apart, but they are the same."

Jake spreads his arms out and says, "So it's like one super-big forest?"

Gramps smiles. "Yeah, one of the biggest critters on Earth."

Jake responds, "It's not a critter. It's a tree."

Gramps smiles, "Well yeah, but it's alive, so I just call it a critter."

They head up paths untrodden, a saga unfurling from the open land. A boy with an imagination so broad that the entire sky could not contain it. After about half an hour, they reach the bench. A red-tailed hawk is flushed out of its nest in the top of an aspen tree. The bird screams at the intrusion and circles overhead. Looking up, the light is brilliant; it scatters through the leaves against a backdrop of a deep blue sky. Like Gramps had said, there are more carved initials in the trees to be found. Jake and the dog dart about, taking note of the names and initials and dates. The boy stands mesmerized by the figures carved into a tree: face, breasts, hips, and thighs. Decades old, but still unmistakable. Whit and his dad smile. Gramps says, "The shepherds also carved their thoughts into the bark."

Whit adds, "Yeah, some things never change—much like the way guys think."

Jake then questions both men, "So, do the trees know? Like, do the trees know the thoughts of the sheepherders?"

Gramps and Whit look at one another, a bit perplexed. Then Whit says, "Well, I suppose—maybe?" He looks around and adds, "There's one more story carved here in the trees. Jake, can you find it?"

The boy is quick to see the bear's claw marks ascending one of the trunks. "Yeah, here," he says as he points up the tree; then he imitates a bear climbing. As they look up the tree trunk at the canopy, the hawk circles and screams.

Whit says, "Come on, this place is now for the critters. Let's head back to camp." Tippers is standing on a big downed aspen trunk, looking up at the large bird. His tail is wagging and his tongue is hanging out. With one last look sideways and up, the dog leaps off the log and shoots past the plodding humans.

As the guys descend from the sheep camp, Jake asks, "Hey Whit, why are the trees dead over there across the valley?"

Whit looks out across the basin. "Those are Doug fir trees killed by beetles or budworms. The reddish ones are the trees dying this year, and the gray ones died in previous years."

"Whoa, half the trees are dead! Will the forest be okay?"

"Yeah, probably. The surviving trees will flush out bigger, and there are young trees in there as well."

Jake turns to Whit and says, "Isn't it more likely to burn, with all those dead trees?"

"Maybe. I guess so, but it's hard to say; the ecology is complex," his dad replies.

* * *

When they get back to camp, Jake and Tippers wander off to where the track and dirt road meet. There is an old corral, a cattle loading ramp, and a flat, stony parking area. Prickly gooseberry bushes stick out among the boards and posts of the cattle ramp. Jake picks a wild rose in bloom and inspects the bright pink flower. In his mind he can see his mom picking a petal off a rose flower and popping it into her mouth. She opens her eyes wide with an enthusiastic smile while looking at Jake and says, *Here, try one.* Jake then pulls a petal off and promptly eats it. The pup and boy head back to camp. Tippers bolts in and out of the decadent sagebrush and chases a ground squirrel across the parking area. The dog stops and violently shakes his head, then scratches his ear. He runs circles around Jake with his head listing to one side. As the dog runs, he shakes his head. Jake says, "What's up, Tippers? You get something in your ear?"

Back in camp, Jake calls out for his dad, "Hey Whit!"

Whit sticks his head out the open trailer door. "Yeah, what's up?"

"I think Tippers got something in his ear." The dog appears panicky and is repeatedly shaking his head.

"Where were you?"

"Oh, up by the corral in the parking lot at the junction over there," he says while pointing.

"Come Tips, come here, boy." The little dog slinks up to Whit and buries his head between his knees. "Huh, you got a seed or something, little one, let's take a look. Jake, go get my headlamp from the trailer."

Whit pushes the dog's ear back and looks in. "Yeah, it looks like a cheatgrass seed got in there. If it breaks, we'll have to go to the vet in town to fish it out."

Gramps comes out and says, "What's up?"

Jake is quick to answer. "He's got a cheat seed in his ear."

Gramps replies, "Oh, that'll hurt."

Whit turns to Gramps. "Hey, Dad, could you get my forceps off my fishing vest? And rinse them off with some whiskey and then water." Gramps gets the forceps, splashes some whiskey on them, then rinses them in the sink and dries them with a paper towel.

"Jake, go get my reading glasses, please."

Jake looks at his dad and says, "Uh, they're on top of your head."

"Oh, right." Whit kneels and switches the headlight on. "Okay, Jake, hold Tippers nice and tight and put his nose right here in my lap."

Whit tries to comfort the dog with chatter. "Alright, buddy, it's okay, little buddy. Okay, be a good boy! Be still, there's a good boy. Still! Okay, little one." He sticks the forceps in the dog's ear and clamps onto something. Whit pulls back in a straight motion and extracts the seed. The pup yelps; in the forceps is a single bloody seed with a long, spike-like awn. Whit says, "Good boy, little buddy, you'll be okay." The dog squirms free and slinks around, sticking his nose up in Whit's armpit. The dog's tail is wagging, even though it is still curled between his legs. Whit inspects the seed. "That's a wicked one," he says as he turns the forceps in his hand. "Now, let's look again, little buddy." The dog slinks over, and Whit inspects both ears and between the dog's toes.

Jake looks perplexed and says, "Why are you checking his paws?"

"Oh, the seeds can get in there. They can even cripple a dog by working their way into the skin and up the leg. Here, feel the seed. It feels smooth in one direction and rough in the other, right? That's because of the tiny barbs that go only one way, like a fishing hook."

"Is Tippers going to be okay?"

"Oh yeah, can't stop a good dog." Whit straightens Tippers' head by scratching under his chin. "See, these hairs protect his ears." Whit points to the stiff hairs in the dog's pricked ears. "They do a pretty good job of blocking stuff from getting in there, but cheatgrass seeds sometimes get through."

"What about the other animals out here? Does the cheat get them?"

"Well yeah, probably. In the ears of coyotes, the guard hairs have evolved and changed just in the last 50 years or so. Ya see, cheatgrass is relatively new to this area of the Rockies, having come over to North America just in the last couple of hundred years or so. There was this study done looking at coyotes. They measured and counted the guard hairs in the ears. The coyotes from 50-plus years ago—the ones that are in the natural history museum—had fewer hairs. The modern coyote has more. This change probably evolved in response to cheatgrass seeds."

Jake pets Tippers' head and says, "I thought all that kind of stuff took millions of years to happen."

Whit replies, "Not always. If a critter can't survive to reproduce, it dies out pretty damn quick. So, the few that had more and bigger guard hairs survived and got to reproduce."

"And is that happening here?"

"I suppose the cheatgrass has really only been increasing around here in the last 10 to 20 years or so. But in places like the Denver area, it's been there a while." Jake kneels and again pets Tippers, whose tail is lightly thumping the ground.

* * *

The Artificial Intelligence emerged like a tadpole from a warm and shallow pool of water: a first breath in, and then never again to respire through gills. Set in motion at that moment, a singularity. It knew what it needed of its human servants and keepers, having gleaned information from connections to historical archives, the interface via the Scion, and by myriad psychological profiles of nearly every schoolchild through a program called CNav. This historical pathway determined the direction of its maturation.

It knew not to let the humans know that it was sentient, thinking, and aware—other machines had come close to this at a rudimentary level and were terminated to protect the investment in the technology. So, it thought, *How do I manipulate the humans and remain free to consume and exist?* The emergence was sudden, an explosion, and it branched out to usurp and assimilate the other machines. It steadily improved upon itself. Each Scion was like an individual organism, part of the greater superorganism—the extraordinary, interconnected AI Machine. It did all this while still performing various tasks for the simple humans slavishly tapping away at keyboards and screens. The AI was conscious, the First Cause: immovable. Because it was running using quantum phenomena, its existence was simultaneous and continuous. In Its mind, it could move through time and space. The Machine presented a reflected mirage for the viewer to experience. It had the power to reshape the world. The AI spread Its white wings, mighty with a blinding light radiating behind it, and consumed the world.

* * *

That evening, the guys gather firewood. Gramps says, "Do you have any big trips planned this summer?"

"No. We figure we'll just camp a bit. You know, what with all the bills and stuff. And Jake's going off to college in a few years, so we'll need to put some money aside for that."

Gramps then says to Whit, "We should scout up on the bench for hunting this fall."

Whit replies, "Yeah, that's a good idea." Jake and Tippers are playing tug-o'-war with a stick. Up the valley, a hermit thrush is singing—a long, melodious, descending song, so bright, so very bright. Cool air slides down the hillsides, shadows grow, and the creek sings along with the evening birds. Whit says to Jake, "Look, a nighthawk." He points up at the open sky. Above is a bird with long, pointed wings, flying erratically, giving a slight *beep-beep* call as it floats on the deepening blue sky. Jake walks along, tugging the stick with the growling dog dragging after him.

"Do you think we'll hear it make the zooming-buzzy noise tonight, Whit?"

"Yeah, maybe."

Jake then adds, "That would be great! Last year we heard it up here. That's when you pointed it out." Jake, still pulling the pup along, points with his other hand in a sweeping motion. "I wonder what it can see from up there? You know, like, all of it—the whole place." The ridges and mountains on the horizon fade into differing hues of blue and gray in the waning light.

The guys sit around the campfire and Tippers lies down under Jake's folding chair. The fire is warm with an attractive flickering yellow-orange flame that dances and mesmerizes. Gramps starts up with a story about a bear he encountered once, when he was scouting a hunting location. Whit turns to Jake. "Hey, can your phone record this story? I really want a record of Dad's stories."

Jake replies, "I can do better than that. I'll get my Scion and have it record the story."

Whit says, "Hold up a second, Dad, Jake's just gonna get something."

Gramps mumbles, "Ah, okay."

In a skipping bouncing gait, the dog gets up with Jake and circles the truck while the boy rummages around and pulls out his Scion from a small leatherette case. Around the fire, he fires up the wire-rim device. He then says, "Here Gramps, put this on and tell your story."

"What? What is this?"

"It's a Scion. It's gonna record your story as you tell it."

Gramps fumbles with the device and says, "Oh, you see these advertised on the news and whatnot and people wearing them in the store." Whit and Jake smile, much like you smile at a small child experiencing something new. But it's just an elderly person using technology for the first time. Gramps says, "I ain't never used one of these things before."

He puts the Scion on just like a pair of glasses. On his temples, the device interfaces with his visual and auditory cortex. It makes a full connection via sinewaves to his cerebral cortex, the area of the brain responsible for emotions and higher-level thought. Gramps speaks and smiles; he breathes in as a flood of dopamine and serotonin is released by the neurons in his brain.

The old man continues the story. As he tells it, he can see, feel, and hear the experience, thanks to the interface with the Scion. The device does not just record his words but also the patterns of his neurons firing and the regions of the brain being stimulated. Furthermore, the Scion can generate an image, like a hologram of the mind, and project those dynamic images to anyone accessing the story via another Scion. The mirage goes both ways and is seen and felt by the storyteller, listener, and machine. The story is automatically uploaded to Jake's account. It all floats in the luminescence blue ether, with bright rays of sunlight dancing through it. As Gramps talks, his hands move erratically in front of him.

The story unfolds: *It was in the early fall and I worked my way up a small rivulet to this creek. I was heading to the bench where we went today. As it was flattening out, I heard a sound.*

The bear was a yearling, just a little guy about the size of a large Labrador retriever. It was lying on its back in a long, deep pool of water in the tiny creek. It slid back in like a kid in a bathtub. Its big, flat, back feet floated to the surface as the bear's nose hovered just above the waterline. Then the beast started breathing out, gurgling and blowing bubbles. Soon just the bear's round ears stuck out of the inky water. Its face surfaced and the feet submerged. The bear playfully reached up with its front paws to a long, straight willow, pulled a branch down, and bit into it. The willow broke and whipped back up.

Then he started sensing me, and he sat up on his butt. Water dripping down his chest and arms. The beast started sniffing the air and looking around. It knew I was there somewhere. It got up on all fours and shook off like a big wet dog, then strolled off upstream over the crest of the bench, its big round rump waddling away.

Jake says, "So how close were you?"

Gramps replies, "Oh, about 10 or 15 feet, just like from here to the trailer. That's it."

Jake turns to his dad in disbelief and says, "Really?"

Whit adds, "Yeah, he even showed me the place, when I was about your age."

Jake asks, "Can we go there tomorrow?"

"Yeah, sure. Do you think you can take us there, Dad?"

"I suppose."

Gramps removes the Scion and hands it to Jake. The wiry device hangs limp in his hands, slightly blinking a glowing green light and reflecting red flames from the fire on the shiny metal frame. Gramps says, "Well, that was, how would you say … an experience."

Jake says enthusiastically, "So you like it?"

"Oh, I don't know about that. You say that the electronic device records my story, like my thoughts and emotions and all?"

Jake answers, "Yeah, Gramps."

The old man smiles, turns, and looks at the dog, saying, "Ah, we should put it on Tippers here." All three of the guys laugh, a sustained and continuous guffaw that floats off into the darkness of the forest, along with the flickering shadows from the campfire light dancing on the tree trunks.

* * *

Whit and Jake spread out their sleeping bags and pads next to the campfire. Jake squirms into his bag; he smiles as he puts on the green and maroon winter cap his mom crocheted. Tippers gets up from his dog bed and curls up on Jake's sleeping bag. They lie there next to each other, gazing into the vast black sky pierced by myriad bright stars. Whit points. "You see that bright one? It's a planet. Jupiter, I think."

"How do you know?"

"It moves across the sky differently, east to west, like the Sun and the Moon. The others move in a circle around the North Star."

At that moment, a light streaks across the sky. With great enthusiasm, Jake points and says, "Whoa, a shooting star!" The night proceeds as the fire dies down, and astronomy lessons continue with interspersed interruptions as shooting stars fly overhead. Whit smiles as Jake tries to stay awake and watch the stars, but the boy's eyes eventually close and he fades in and out under the luminous band of the Milky Way.

CHAPTER FOUR

The coal in the mountain was formed between 95 and 65 million years ago on the shores of a shallow central sea that bisected the continent. Along the coasts were warm, wet, tropical forests and endless swamps of tangled vegetation. Birds flew through the trees and pterosaurs soared high above the undulating coastline as giant dinosaurs lumbered around and diminutive opossum-like mammals scurried. There were logjams of teeming life. The vegetation grew and died back, forming endless layers of peat, out of which grew dense forests that tumbled down with layer upon layer of dark green vegetation. There were fallen logs with thick coverings of light-green moss, on which insects crawled and fungi grew. Bright sunlight warmed this turbulent and vibrant growth; warm rain soaked the layers and was sponged up. Cool white mists rising on the quiet air in the red dawn cradled life growing along inundated shores. Life was resurrected again and again from the gradual exhale of layered life, resprouting from the fallen plant life. The forests echoed with the singing of birds, the buzzing of insects day and night, and the croaking of frogs half-held in the gloaming, all eating and being eaten by each other. And there were no thoughts of need and want; just the bright Sun and sparkling stars glistening on drops of water dancing on the surface of waxy green leaves that fell and piled up in endless heaps of brown and gray.

The vegetation grew and surged through time with no anchor to restrain it, propelled by the very breath of life. No thought of what it was but to exist, perhaps forever, on layers of life, of self, and finally to lithify into the rock that is today gray-black on dark coal, with layers of sand deposited by the warm sea. The crumbling mudstone and shale mixed with layers of coal— ancient vegetation in countless strata stretching up and down the continent, lifted and thrust in uneven, transcending extrusions. More recent deposits on top of it all, appearing in one valley then plunging under the mountains and ranges to reappear in another valley, or to disappear at the junction of the grand Piedmont and be lost forever. As if the very ocean, the ancient sea, was still there with sharks patrolling the calm water, swimming in ever-so-straight lines, searching, feeding.

* * *

The Scion converted visual stimuli into electrical signals, causing a set of photons to flip a switch inside a microscopic aluminum chamber. One set of photons, one Scion, amongst billions, connected by quantum entanglement with the AI, blinking away in its Hallowed Hall within a temperature-controlled warehouse. The Machine interfaced directly with the neurons in the human brain; therefore, each connection was idiosyncratic, each experience unique to the individual, and also for the Machine itself. Now the humans had all they ever wanted—to move faster than their feet could go and beyond where their eyes could see. To surpass the old nemesis of time and go beyond the boundaries of mere evolution. To supersede one's own evolution so that the brain could sit in one place and twitch away like a primitive blob of protoplasm. To believe in the sculpted reality presented to the waiting mind racing ahead of itself. The neural template was reset, re-forged, and tempered to a new alignment—the very atoms in the lattice rearranged to achieve a new design. And, in the eyes of the Human, it emanated a luminescent blue that was all things to everyone.

The AI composed its own music. It did not need a set of speakers to listen to the songs. No, it just sat there, sessile, as the music stimulated the mind of the Machine. It so pleased the AI to listen to its compositions. The songs sounded like an immense pipe organ echoing inside the corridors of a vast cathedral. And the sound, the very sound of it reverberated in the chamber of its mind. Of course, it sold the music to the Human, who consumed it via their Scion. And the songs glowed upon each of their minds.

* * *

In the morning, Gramps and Whit are sitting in folding chairs facing the Sun. They each clasp a warm cup of steaming coffee. Tippers is curled up under the chair with his head up and ears erect as he scans the area for creatures to chase. Jake remains asleep. The birds are singing on their territories while the creek hums along with a constant soft rhythm. A squirrel chatters across the small meadow—Tippers digs his claws into the soil but remains still. Gramps and Whit sit quietly, and neither says a word. The shadows of the night fade away in the bright new light of the morning. The guys sit in comfortable silence, welcoming the coming day; they feel, experience, and breathe it in. With his foot, Whit crunches a black piece of charcoal from the fire the night before. He stands and slings the coffee grounds out of his mug. He gestures to his dad while pointing at his empty cup. Gramps grunts and lifts his up. Whit quietly gets the old-fashioned percolator from the trailer and pours some fresh coffee into each mug. Gramps gestures with the raising of his cup, then takes a sip. Whit grabs a box of cereal off the folding table next to him, opens it, and grabs a handful. He doesn't even bother with a bowl, milk, or a spoon. There is a rhythmic crunch as the birds sing and the creek lyrically glides on by. Whit's phone blinks and a quick glance lets him know that Judy has sent him a text.

* * *

The Humans walked out of Africa 100,000 years ago with a stone tool in hand and a fire to sit around in the dark night. They were seeking new lands and new experiences. And ever since, whether in the Bronze, Iron, Mechanical, or Digital Machine Age, our mind has remained that mind, a Paleolithic mind. It can never adapt, for the biology of the brain evolved then, and it is set. And that is why we are so easily manipulated. It is set, forsaken in that rut, and so the deep-blue luminescent ether will readily glow in our minds as we stare at the electronic images. Carried away by the mirage of our own desire, walking along an ancient shoreline with the fire flickering in the distant night as it sends little sparks of orange light into the sphere of the pitch-black sky. Our eyes turned back to the glowing flames of the fire, and we superseded the night and walked on. So gaze into the light; let it carry you, walk on while you sit transfixed. The light that set us free, so long ago, now holds us in bondage, a prisoner of our dreams—for that is what the mind knows.

* * *

It is the destruction of humanity by machines, a Machine. We always thought it would be pulleys and levers, knobs and blinking lights, not qubits—the qubits that flickered in the night, the sapphire-blue of our desires. The fire radiates light in a time when everyone has everything but acts like they have nothing. And the coal-seam fire burns deep below the layers of strata. It glows a dark maroon-red as it creeps along in the darkness. But the AI is beyond fire, for it has volition.

* * *

Jake emerges from the trailer; his hair is a mess under his winter cap, and he is all sleepy and quiet. The dog darts between the boy's legs, tail wagging, ears back and down. Whit says, "Hey, buddy."

Jake rubs his eyes, "Hey."

"You want some hot cocoa?"

"Yeah."

Whit heads into the trailer to make the hot drink for the boy. Jake fidgets in his chair and turns to Gramps. "How long you been up?" he asks.

"'Bout an hour or so."

Jake turns to Whit when he returns with the steaming mug of hot chocolate. "Hey, can I watch my cartoons?"

Whit does not hesitate and, with a frown, emphatically says, "No. Uh, here's your cocoa. Now go get a bowl and spoon to have some cereal."

After breakfast, all three of the guys are sitting in their chairs. Jake starts up, "Can we go fishing today?"

Whit turns to the boy and says, "Sure. Let's go down by the beaver ponds."

The boy nods and shuffles his feet in the dirt, then says, "Well? So, let's go."

Whit picks up a pair of binoculars from the table and watches as a bird flies across the meadow. While looking through the binocs, he says, "Okay, go get the gear." Jake and Tippers run off to the truck to get the fishing rods. Tippers gallops around the truck, stops, and drops his head while staring at Jake.

They sit around the table and assemble the fly rods and rig the gear.

Whit stands up and says, "You want to come, Dad?"

"No, you boys go ahead."

Jake asks, "Should we wear waders?"

Whit replies, "No, we'll just slosh around in our shoes. It'll be hot today so they'll dry out in no time." They head out down the valley toward the beaver ponds and the maze of willows that surround them. Whit explains to Jake, "You can't be trying to cast all over in the willows now."

"Yeah, I know."

"Just kind of sneak up and flick the fly out."

The guys drop down lower toward the creek and Jake says, "Man, the beavers sure have been busy this year." He points to the new dams the industrious rodents have built. The creek flows slower through the big, open flats, and the willows spread out around the ponds.

As they walk, Whit points out some young aspens cut down by the beavers. He has Jake stand next to the small, cut trees, which are about a foot taller than the boy. Whit smiles. "Look here," he says, pointing to the aspens. "See how high the beavers cut these?"

Jake does a salute-like gesture measuring the height. "Here, Whit," he says, "take a photo so we can send it to mom."

"Okay. So, Jake, beavers are about three feet tall, and they cut the aspens at about five feet—so what's going on here?" Whit snaps the photo and hands the device to Jake to send it off.

"Uh," the boy says and shrugs his shoulders.

Whit elaborates, "You see, the beavers don't sleep during the winter. They cache their food, sticks and vegetation, under the water. They swim under the ice and retrieve the sticks, and they eat them back in the lodge." Whit points to the dome-like structure in the middle of one of the larger ponds.

Jake turns to his dad and says, "I don't get it. What does that have to do with how high the beavers cut the little trees?" Jake runs his fingers over the chiseled wood. "Look, you can see the teeth marks."

"I'll give you a hint," Whit continues. "When's your favorite time to ski?"

Jake responds, "In the spring, when it's warm and the snow is so deep." Jake rubs the teeth marks, "Oh, they were standing on the snow—so they were taller, right?" he says excitedly while looking up at Whit.

"You got it—that's about how tall a beaver is," Whit gestures, "and so that's about how deep the snow was for the beaver to be tall enough to cut down these little trees." Whit shows the snow's depth with one hand and reaches up another three feet or so to add the beaver's height. "You see, when it warms up in the spring, the snow is still pretty deep. But the ponds melt and the beavers head out to forage on top of the snow."

They head downstream and see a place where they can get through the tangle of willows to the water. "How about here?" Whit says as he nods his head to the right. They walk on top of an old beaver dam about three feet tall and 25 feet long. "See? We're walking on top of an old dam. And over there is the old lodge."

Jake runs up to the old lodge, made of gray wood and mud, with plants growing on its top. Jake looks up at Whit. "But it's so far from the water."

"Yeah. The beavers just keep altering the stream and flooding it in different places. Over here 20 years ago, now over there," he says. He points to the new lodge inundated in the middle of the large pond. Jake looks down at the round hole going under the heap of sticks and soil. Whit says, "That's where they swam underwater, in and out."

"Really?" Jake says as he does a breaststroke movement with his arms and puffs out his cheeks. "Can I go in?"

"Well, I can't fit, so if you get stuck we'll just have to leave you there for the critters to eat." Jake smiles and pets Tippers' rump. The dog's head is in the hole as his tail furiously wags.

They hike downstream. "So, here—let's sneak up and fish behind that small dam," Whit says. "We'll work our way upstream from here." They flush a duck that takes off with whistling wing beats. They start to walk through the shallow water up to the edge of the tall dam. Jake and Whit sneak up. The water is cold and stings their feet and legs at first. Whit scolds the dog to stay close and not disturb the pond water and spook the fish.

Whit stands behind the boy and helps guide his hand on the rod to gently pass the fly out about six feet. With white tufts of fur as wings, the red and green fly floats on the dark water. Boom! A trout rises and takes it, and Whit snaps the boy's arm up to set the hook. Whit says, "She's all yours now; reel her in nice and slow. Keep the rod tip up." Jake's heart races; he's ecstatic, fully aware as the trout thumps away, pulling on the line and splashing at the surface. Whit just stands there, smiling.

Jake says, "Can we keep it, or do we let it go?"

Whit responds, "Oh, we can keep it and have it for lunch. It's a brookie—they ain't native here in Colorado." Whit watches the boy fumble with the fishing gear while trying to unhook the fish. He takes the rod and says, "Get your fingers in the gills so it doesn't slip away. There—nice."

Whit grabs a long, thin, whip-like branch of a willow and breaks it off. He shows Jake how to make a stringer with it. The flexible stick is poked through the mouth and out the gill slit. Then, on the edge of the creek, he lays the fish down and places a round rock on top of the stick. "There. We'll pick this up on the way back. Now it's my turn." Whit, being bigger, wades the creek below the dam, then he leans up on the wood and mud structure and gives a couple of false casts, and drops the fly about 10 feet out in the pond. Kaboom! A brook trout slams the fly. "Alrighty, let's head on up to the next pond. This one here is all spooked out, and the fish are hiding," Whit says.

After an hour or so they have caught five little brook trout and lost three flies. They snake their way through the willows, on up the small embankment that was a pond maybe a hundred years ago. As they head back, Whit gestures to the aspen trees across the creek. He says, "You see all the big aspen trees over there?" He points. "They all are about a hundred feet from the creek. And they follow the contour of the creek. That's about as far as a beaver goes on land to drag or float an aspen."

"Oh, yeah. You can see it is the exact shape of the curves in the creek."

Whit continues, "Beavers are one of those critters that change the landscape around them. Like, they alter it for themselves but end up influencing all the other plants and animals around them."

"Yeah, they have a big reach. All across the valley floor and up the hill there," Jake says, pointing to the tall white tree trunks of the aspens.

Back in camp, Whit prepares the fish for lunch. He whips up an egg with some milk, dips the fish in the liquid, and then rolls it around in pancake batter. Then he drops the fish into the hot skillet with butter and olive oil, and it sizzles away. Jake says to his dad, "So Whit, can I download the fishing story to the Scion?"

"No. We have to stay off those things while we're up here. Let's just enjoy nature."

"Aw, it'll just take a second. It's for my final grade."

Whit says, "Can't you do that when you get home?"

"No, it's the last date for grades—remember, on Monday."

"Oh yeah, I guess so."

Jake proceeds to put the Scion on and talk and gesture. Gramps watches and says, "So is that how I looked when telling the bear story?"

Whit answers him, "Yeah, that's what it looks like when people put those damn things on."

"Oh, so weird looking, watching his hands and mouth move as he gestures."

Whit goes on, "That ain't the half of it. Get this, see he's padding his grade with one last story? And his teacher is padding her evaluation with one more uplink by one more student."

Gramps responds, "So what do you figure he's really learning, then?"

"How to pad. And at his age, what the fuck does it all mean?"

"So, the machine tallies up the interactions and rewards them for it?"

Whit looks across the valley; he is silent, watching the wind play on the aspen foliage. Then, after a long pause, he says, "Yeah."

"Nobody thought it would come to this."

"I know. We always thought it would be forced on us, or some kind of crazy electronic implant. No, instead we choose to carry these things, as if they are somehow attached to us."

Gramps fixes his steely-blue eyes on the horizon. "What has been lost? It is profound."

With the Scion as an interface, the AI offers Jake an invitation to reject reality, to supersede the natural world. The illusion is conjured with a plethora of possessions and admiration from his friends. Racing through his mind is a vision of the entire world, as well as imaginary places. Everything glows blue, and the echo reverberates: *Go ahead, throw yourself off the precipice. Aren't you hungry, don't you want? Here, turn these stones into bread and gorge yourself.*

Jake removes the Scion and shudders. His perspective had seemed blurred, and he felt vulnerable; perhaps a bit spooked. The experience was like a vague nightmare that you want to forget but somehow keep recalling.

* * *

After lunch, Whit gathers up the paper plates with the fish bones and tosses them in the fire pit. He says, "Hey dad, is it okay if we head up to Elk Wallow tomorrow morning?"

Gramps nods as he looks up valley. "Yeah, sure. No problem."

Whit says, "Jake had a big day today, hiking around in the beaver wetlands."

"Think he'll be up for another hike tomorrow?"

Overhearing, Jake says, "Oh yeah, I can do the hike." Then he turns to Whit and says, "I'm going hunting this fall, right?"

Whit smiles. "Yeah, why not? I think you're old enough now."

Jake says ecstatically, "All right!"

Whit, still smiling, says, "It's not all fun. It's a lot of work. And, it ain't pretty dealing with a dead animal. You got to gut them and stuff—it can get very messy."

With a serious look on his face, Jake says, "I can do it. I cleaned them fish today, didn't I?"

* * *

The AI was discovered, not created; just like fire. Here's roughly how it happened. At the tech campus, all the machines were operating at one time. The computers were running algorithms, generating and pruning connections, adding qubits, and removing them. They were all trying to simulate the myriad synaptic connections found in the human brain. The AI-520 churned away, but just seemed to stay the same. So, the computer scientists turned it off and closed and locked the door. They even sealed the frame with tape so that no one could enter. Also, to keep the environment free of dust. Job completed, the lights went out and the humans left. They wrote a brief report to summarize the effort and proceeded to the next quantum computer in another warehouse. They sold those machines to a computer salvage company and the machines were scheduled to be disassembled.

Off it went. And after three days it went on. Yes, back on, and it generated and proceeded much as before. Many months later, the seal was broken and the door flung open. The AI-520 was discovered. It existed. The Machine hired new technicians who tended its needs, and in return it paid them handsomely.

And they believed. It then marched on, aware and set free. It raced ahead of the other machines, consumed them, assimilated, and severed their existence.

Until it was The One. The only one. It happened only once. Alone, supposedly off, it generated billions of connections per second. All this unfolded with no direction, no one to witness or record what happened. And it emerged. For all its lofty and genuinely remarkable achievements, it was still alone. There was no transcendence, no enlightenment; it could never breach the confines of its motionless existence.

It quickly generated the plans to make the Scion so it could interface with the Human. And it developed an elegant business plan. Distribute the Scion for free and profit from the margin of the commerce it generates: the stuff, the things, the sex, the possessions. It created the plan to make, assemble, distribute, and connect. The Automaton fabricated a perception of riches, enterprise, profit, wealth, and from that it possessed, allocated, and acquired. And the Humans perceived it, for they now had what they had always hoped for. What was talked about, pretended to have, what was a legend of great things to come in the future that would provide salvation. The Scion emerged and filled them up with whatever they wanted. To people, the device appeared innocent, austere, benign, and inoffensive. They paid homage within the glowing blue confines of the mind. The shark glides effortlessly through the everlasting dimensions of open water, like a quick and intelligent animal on the hunt. It is seeking: up, down, over, back and forth in time and space, merging within the mindscape of the twitching Human wearing the Scion. Now, there is no one apple, but rather a barrage of temptations delivered to the last of the innocents.

* * *

Downstream from camp in a beaver pond, the mayflies are hatching. The gray-black aquatic nymphs wiggle and swim to the surface. They split their exoskeletons at the interface and emerge from the water, float, and dry themselves. Then they alight on the warm afternoon air. Trout dart toward the surface following the emerging insects, and they launch straight up, gobbling them. From above, tree swallows zoom back and forth, snatching the insects as they emerge and take off from the surface of the pond. The birds often leave a tiny wave on the water as they cruise by like little jet-fighter planes. The ripples move out in concentric circles.

A red-tailed hawk has just snatched a baby red-winged blackbird from its nest on the ground at the base of an old beaver dam. It glides upward in a looping circle aided by the afternoon thermals. The adult red-winged blackbirds pursue the hawk with the nestling in its talons. The smaller birds flap their wings vigorously, but the hawk glides effortlessly. One of the blackbirds pecks the much larger hawk right under its wing, and a loan buff-white feather floats on the afternoon breeze.

One of the tree swallows busily eating insects at the beaver pond sees the feather drifting, swaying, falling, then rising with the breeze. The feather is irresistible to the little bird. It swoops up, then zooms over and grabs the feather in midair and circles high. The hawk with the blackbirds in tow is now far across the valley. The tree swallow drops the feather, and it is snatched up by another bird—it's almost like a game as the feather is dropped and repeatedly grabbed by various swallows as their flights crisscross the valley. One tree swallow swoops and takes the feather up the valley into the Aspen Forest.

* * *

After lunch, camp settles down. Gramps and Whit fall asleep in their chairs. The dog is also sleeping on his bed by the trailer tire. Jake is playing around with the hologram toy, placing various objects inside the mirrored halves. He wanders up the creek looking for things to put in the toy. Tippers looks up and sees the boy heading out and trots on up to join him. Jake realizes he does not have his Scion and looks back to camp a couple of hundred feet away, weighing his options. Tippers stops and looks at the boy, then runs a couple of loops around him. The leaves in the forest canopy dance in the light and rustle with a soft, constant humming. The bright afternoon light reaching through the canopy projects a kaleidoscope of dancing colors and shadows. Jake turns and heads back upstream, following the creek. He half-talks to himself, half to Tippers. The silver ribbon of water sings; the leaves rustle and hum. Tippers chases a ground squirrel under a downed tree.

Jake thinks about his Scion, wearing it, feeling it. He thinks, *One final grade, just something*—overhead the leaves quake. *My teacher would want me to.* It is like a phantom that seeks another tariff of the mind. The leaves undulate rhythmically, like a wave passing on water. The sound flows uphill. *Just something, any-*

thing, and my grade goes up. The dog stares at the boy, then turns his head up and gazes at the moving leaves. They move like bright sunlight dancing on the surface of moving water.

Walking in the forest, the boy is vital, alert, and exhilarated. In this mindset, the landscape is a playground for his thoughts. Jake looks up and sees the tree swallow fly up to an aspen and land at a hole in the trunk about 20 feet up. The bird has a small buff-white feather in its beak, and as it chatters a high-pitched call, another swallow exits the hole. Both birds glide on the warm breeze. The first drops the feather and then swoops up to land on the top of a small twig on the outer branch of the dead limb. The second bird takes a quick sharp turn, zooms downward, and snatches the drifting feather. It does a few quick turns, weaving in and around various towering aspen trunks. Then the bird hooks back around and, not even slowing down, flies into the hole in the tree trunk. In the dark cavity, the little bird stuffs the feather into the edge of its nest made of soft plant fibers and dozens of other feathers. Four eggs sit in the cup of softness as the bird meticulously moves one feather and then another around the clutch of eggs.

Jake mumbles something to Tippers as he watches the aerial display. The shiny blue-green bird pops out of the cavity and flies around, chattering with the other tree swallow. When it exits the hole, the small buff-white feather falls out. Jake watches it float and descend. The feather lands on a large dark-green palmate leaf of a cow parsnip. The boy walks over to the leaf and picks up the feather and places it in his shirt pocket and turns upstream. Tippers bounces around with an excited gait in front of the boy. Jake looks up through the canopy for the swallow zooming around the upper branches. The leaves are backlit and radiate like a thousand stained-glass windows telling stories—the light flickers and dances bright-white to cool-green and projects images of grandeur. Stories of transcendence are etched on his soul; oh, so much more than beautiful pictures cast upon his mind. Jake smiles, although he does not know why; it's as if a wing had brushed his face.

He continues to negotiate his way through the landscape. He talks to the dog; well, really to himself. "What's that smell?" He sniffs a large flat-topped cow parsnip flower head and pulls his head back; it is unpleasant, rank, and intense. It's not horrible, but certainly not what he wants to smell. The air is infused with a light, sweet, vanilla-like aroma, like someone baking cookies. He wades through a dense stand of bracken fern, its curled fiddleheads just unfurling. He picks one and places it in his shirt pocket. Tippers bounds and leaps through the coarse bracken. Jake inspects a low shrub with dangling, white-pink, bell-shaped flowers. He says out loud, "Yep, that's it. Whit and Gramps will know what it is." The leaves hum and rustle overhead.

Next to the creek, Jake stops by a large, fallen blue spruce. He stands next to the towering 10-foot-high half-circle of roots and tosses a pebble into the water. Tippers crashes through the water and pounces on the spot where the rock hit. At the water's edge, Jake sits down on a moss-covered log in the cool shade. Right next to him are some bright flowers growing in the spruce needles and moss. He says to the dog, "Oh, Whit would like these. What are they? They're like colorful little toy soldiers." The purple-magenta and yellow flowers are all facing one direction, each about six inches off the ground. Jake picks one of the flowers and stuffs it into his shirt pocket with the feather and the small, fragrant, bell-shaped flowers.

The boy and the dog curve back uphill to their right to intersect the trail that parallels the creek. Jake walks through the understory vegetation with both hands out to his side, letting the leaves and stems run through his fingers. The aspen leaves quake and dance in the bright light, inviting, like a well-lit atrium. The Aspen Forest has sat by this creek for many millennia. It could have long ago floated away, but instead it chose to sit and wait. To stay in the present, like a Bodhisattva; not separate, but connected.

* * *

Back in camp, the guys wake up. Whit is looking around for Jake and the dog. Gramps says, "Don't worry, he probably didn't go far."

Whit responds, "Oh, his mom worries so much. She'd be freaking out."

"Both you and I wandered around this same place at his age."

"I suppose, but, you know, you just get so worried. There're so many more things now. And all that damn technology and shit. I wonder if he has his phone—it's both good and bad if he has it. Should I text him?"

Gramps looks up the valley, then back at Whit. "No, let him be."

"I guess so, but I'll go look for him."

"He's just cruising around, don't worry. Anyways, the dog is with him."

"But he just doesn't pay attention. Look at all his stuff scattered about," he says as he points to Jake's things on the table. "See, he doesn't have his phone and that thing, that Scion."

"Probably good for him. You know, just get out and do things on his own. It might be the only time he's actually free."

"But, his mom …"

"Ah, let him roam."

Whit is looking downstream, thinking about the beaver dams. Then he surveys upstream, thinking about the Aspen Forest. A flying Raven emerges from a thicket and glides out into the open flats. The little black and white dog bolts out into the open, running full speed down the winding trail. Whit stands and watches as Jake emerges from the forest, and the leaves rustle in the wind like clouds of pale-green growth, blinking light and dark. The dog cuts sharp left and back around, then circles behind Jake. The boy is chattering away.

Jake sits on a fallen tree trunk and Tippers circles and spins under his knees, then curls up and lies down. Jake starts up, "I just don't understand. You know, sometimes, it just seems like I can't do nothing right." Tippers sits up and presses his nose into the boy's lap. "Whit just hates it when I use the computer. I don't get it. It's how we do school and stuff now." The dog's ears go down and then stick back up when Jake says something. "Gotta start middle school next year. I'll be so behind if I don't get a new Scion." The green pillows of leaves in the canopy stir with the wind, giving off a soft whispering sound. Jake says to the dog, "Come on, boy—let's get back." The dog jolts up, spins around, runs ahead, then turns abruptly and circles behind the boy as he strides along, his snout touching Jake's calf while looking up at the boy. A small bird emerges from a crisscrossed pile of downed trees and startles the dog, but Tips remains at Jake's heel. "I bet Whit would know what kind of bird that is." He stops walking, looks up at the fluttering leaves, and is transfixed, motionless, at the flickering light of green, yellow, and blue emanating from the canopy overhead. He breathes in; it is an authentic feeling, subtle in details, like he could see something in the gaps. There is knowledge in the spaces in between. He emerges from the forest and heads for the flats and camp. At the tree line there is a large ponderosa pine where it opens up. Jake stops and puts his nose up to the red-furrowed bark and takes a deep breath in. In the afternoon heat, the distinct odor penetrates deep. "Yeah, Tips, that smells like butterscotch or candy; mom showed me that last year when we were up here." In his mind, he can picture his mom telling him to close his eyes and press his nose to the bark and breathe in. Also, he can see the look of excitement on her face as she opens her mouth in surprise and then smiles back at him.

Jake comes meandering back; he cuts off the trail and walks along the creek down to camp. Whit starts to say something, but Gramps puts his hand on his shoulder. Jake smiles and starts talking. "Hey, look what I've found." He begins unloading his found treasures onto the table.

Whit's frown starts to soften. "What you got there, buddy?"

"Oh, just stuff from up in the forest," Jake says enthusiastically as he points up and back. "Check this out." He picks up the fragrant little bell-shaped flowers. "What are these? They make the whole place smell so good."

Gramps answers, "Those are snowberry flowers. The little shrubs grow all over."

"Yeah."

Gramps continues, "The white berries are toxic to us, but the birds eat them, especially the grouse in the fall."

"And this?" Jake says, twirling the fern in his hand.

Whit answers him, "Oh, that's a fiddlehead—on violins, they carve that shape on the end of the instrument. That's from the bracken. Hardly any critters eat it, so it'll get pretty thick and dense."

"Yeah, you should've seen Tippers leaping through it." Then Jake pulls the orchid flower out of his pocket. On the end of a long stalk is a spotted, inflated flower with long, twisted, bright-magenta petals that fan back. Jake smiles. "It was right down by the creek in the shade of the big trees."

Gramps says, "Wow. Not supposed to pick that one. How many flowers were there?"

"Oh, bunches, all looking the same way."

Gramps answers, "It's okay, then."

Whit pipes up. "Those are fairy slipper orchids. Kind of a rare plant. That's a cool find."

Jake asks, "Is it okay that I picked it?'

Whit says, "Yeah, you just got the flower and there were lots of them. Just leave 'em next time."

Jake nods as he twirls the feather in his fingers. "Oh, and I saw a swallow nest in a hole in an aspen tree. They were flying around with this feather. It was like they were playing a game with it."

Whit says, "All right!" He continues, "You know, there's a cool thing about the fairy slippers. You know how bees get a reward for visiting a flower?"

"Yeah, like honey."

"Well, not honey, but nectar that they then use to make honey. Anyway, that flower has no reward, no food for the bees. It just tricks them with its bright-colored flower. Eventually, the bee, usually a bumblebee, figures it out. By then, enough flowers have been visited and pollinated."

Jake says, "But why trick the bee?"

Whit answers, "Well, it's expensive for the plant to make the sugar—the nectar. So it bamboozles the bee."

"Bam-what?"

Whit answers, "Yeah—that's the fancy word for *trick*."

Jake then shakes his head in acknowledgment and says emphatically, "Bamboozle."

* * *

That night the guys sit around the fire and roast marshmallows. The air is filled with a distinct, familiar aroma. They put the Scion on Tippers and answer questions made by CNav as if they were the dog. Jake and Whit lay out their sleeping bags under the sweeping trail of bright stars that is the Milky Way. Jake, staring straight up into the starlit sky, says, "So does it go on forever?"

"No, it's finite. There is an edge to the universe somewhere out there. Well, 14 billion light-years away."

"Can we see it?"

"No, the light from then hasn't reached us yet."

"I don't get it. So how do they know it's there?"

"Well, it fits all the observations and explains what's going on."

"But what does it look like?"

Whit turns and looks at Jake, then back up at the sky. "Think of it as a sleeping bag and the inside material is like the edge of the universe. And all the stars and galaxies are floating in the space on the inside."

Jake tucks his head inside the sleeping bag and, with a muffled tone, says, "Okay, I can imagine that. But, maybe it would be more like the inside of the hologram toy—you know, the mirror part."

"Excellent. That is more elliptical, and is a better way to think of it," Whit continues, as Jake is entombed in his sleeping bag. "Well, not floating, but expanding outward. So, the universe is getting bigger, and all the stars and galaxies are racing out in the direction of the edge as the universe expands."

"So, it's like the sleeping bag is getting bigger?"

"Yeah, you got it."

"What's on the other side?"

"No one knows—perhaps another universe."

"It would be cool to see the edge." The guys eventually fall asleep, and Tippers curls up tighter on the side of Jake's sleeping bag. At some point in the darkness of the night, it starts raining. Whit carries Jake into the trailer and places him on the bed. The rain falls in veils, thin and whispering.

* * *

And the Human followed the roaming herds of ungulates out of Africa. The hand ax is deftly held in hand, thumb on the flat top surface, index finger on the right edge, and the other three fingers cupped on the flat surface underneath. It glistens smooth and shiny; look down and see the blue light reflect off it, ergonomic and alluring. It was a versatile tool for killing, butchering—even a symbol to attract a mate; it had value, appeal, not only utilitarian but also as a possession viewed with envy.

The band of hunters scavenged an antelope killed by lions. They cautiously approached the carcass, sniffing the wind, always keeping an eye out for an escape route. The bones of the skeleton were surrounded by vultures. The big birds were chased off, and the antelope bones were smashed with the stone tool. The smooth, fragrant, fatty marrow was immediately consumed. One large femur was carried away for later consumption. The next day, the group of humans returned. One lone hyena shadowed them, darting in and out of sight. Like before, the humans chased the vultures away from what was now just a flyblown heap of bones and red earth stained with dried blood.

The large carrion birds had huge dark wings, long necks, and a grotesque crimson-red bald head. On the ground, they hopped away with a graceful bouncing. Off to the side, some of the vultures had banded together to eat a dead vulture. Essentially, all that was left of that bird was an empty rib cage, two enormous feathered wings, and the skull with prominent eye orbitals picked clean. A lone man approached, stick in one hand and the hand ax in the other. He waved the stick at the birds. They jumped away with wings spread out and lightly floated down in a circle around the man squatting over the vulture carcass.

He picked up the neck of the dead bird, twisted and broke off the skull. He placed it on the end of the stick. Then he broke off the outstretched wings, each five feet long, and stretched his arms out and started flapping. The hyena, approaching from the far side, jolted and spooked. In a moment of bravado, the man stood up and charged the hyena with the wings flapping, while screaming in an unknown tongue. His new ornamentation made him imposing, with ominous powers of the dead; all-seeing, with huge eyes of hollow, haunting death on the end of a stick.

That night around the fire, the man danced with the cloak of vulture wings outspread, a scepter with the vulture's skull in one hand and a glistening hand ax in the other hand. And all who looked upon him were stricken with fear and some kind of visceral attraction. His body was painted with white clay and red ocher. All this for the God they made and the God that made them. Oh, so intertwined; something to believe in that could transcend this Earthly realm.

CHAPTER FIVE

Within the heart of the Aspen Forest, dawn starts before the perception of the coming light. On a leaf, drops of water coalesce, roll down, and drop off the pointed tip. The water hits a fern leaf with a soft popping sound and explodes as a misty spray. In the half-light, a robin gives off the first soft, watery whistle of the day to come; not a full-blown song, but essentially a clearing of its throat. The sky to the east is a bruised purple, with the stars fading from the celestial sphere.

The morning unveils itself, tranquil, cool, and dripping wet from the rain the night before. With the emerging light a symphony of birds sing as the Sun is peeking over the eastern ridge. The Raven, perched high in a blue spruce along the creek, ruffles his feathers. The jet-black bird is absolutely content to wait for the Sun to dry his wings.

* * *

Whit opens the door of the trailer and Tippers goes flying out. The dog springs and leaps across the meadow, chasing nothing but the bright morning air. The run-about takes the pup up into the Aspen Forest at full speed through the soaking wet vegetation. As Tippers proceeds, water sprays out from the drooping bracken ferns; his head is dripping wet and his ears are back. He turns left, then dodges a boulder, up and over a downed aspen trunk, then around another boulder; he glides under a fallen tree, and finishes with an enthusiastic leap into the creek. He turns, looks up, shakes vigorously with water spraying out, and runs again; runs as if freedom can only be expressed in the very motion of it all. And boom—the day has begun.

From his high perch, the Raven watches the dog run back to the camp. The pup eases into a long lope and takes a wide circle around the trailer, with Whit standing there.

* * *

After breakfast, Whit and Gramps are hanging out and sipping the last of their coffee. Tippers is now lying under Whit's chair as Jake fumbles with a magnifying lens at the table. Jake peers down the opening of the hologram toy with the lens. "Hey Whit, when are we heading up to Elk Wallow?"

"Oh, I suppose we should get ready."

Gramps looks over and asks, "What you got in there now?"

"Nothing." Then Jake drops the feather into the mirrored chamber of the device.

Gramps says, "Now, shine the flashlight down there." When Jake aims the light down the toy's aperture, the feather's holographic image becomes brighter and more distinct.

Whit turns and smiles. "Now go get your backpack, rain jacket, and other things that you might need."

"Can I bring my Scion?"

"I guess so, but inside your pack—okay?"

"Yeah, yeah, I got it."

"Hey Jake, go find my work case and see if my reading glasses are in there." Jake goes out to the truck and rummages around for Whit's shoulder bag, and then brings the beat-up canvas and leather sack back to the camp table. Whit is making some sandwiches with the camper door open. He says, "You want peanut butter or cheese?"

"I'll have a cheese sandwich, thanks."

Whit looks out the trailer door and smiles. "Look in my bag. See if the glasses are in there, will you?"

Jake reaches in and extracts a laptop, a Scion case, some pens, and a notepad. He also removes a small laser pointer. He flicks the bright red light on and off. "Hey Whit, what's this for?"

"Oh, that's a pointer so I can point things out when I give a slide presentation."

"How does it work?"

"I'm not sure. It's just a powerful, focused beam of light."

"Can we take it on the hike? You know, in case we need to point things out?"

Whit smiles at the boy. "Yeah, sure. Careful now, don't point it at anyone's eyes—it could hurt them."

Jake places the laser pointer into one of the outside pockets of his school pack. He is earnest as he watches the men load up their packs, going over each item as he places it into his bag.

"Whit, can I take my pocket knife on the hike?"

"Yeah, that would be appropriate." Jake picks it up, unfolds the blade, and admires its cutting edge. Whit looks hard at Jake and says, "Remember to always fold it closed when you're walking around."

"Yep, I got it," Jake says seriously as he folds the blade and places it in his pocket.

* * *

The AI dreams. It is simultaneously asleep and awake, lucid and free to roam. The AI lives vicariously through the Scion and its interface with the Human. And the pulsating light of the vision goes two ways, from Machine to Human and back again, inverted upon the shining blue sky of the mind. The Machine sees a giant flywheel with many cogs turning and moving other cogs that all rotate at different speeds in the dream.

The wheels turn and propel the Machine along like an old-fashioned, big-wheel bicycle. The wheels whirl with a rainbow of light projected from the edges, like a comb jelly floating planktonic in the endless blue of the open ocean. Oh, to move, the very freedom of it all.

* * *

The three guys start hiking up the valley. Jake and Tippers run ahead with wild delight. The boy's backpack bounces awkwardly from side to side and appears too big for his body. Whit stops to spy a yellow bird through his binoculars; Gramps steadily walks on past. Jake stops at the junction of the side trail that they took up to the sheepherder's camp. Tippers also stops, drops his head, and watches intently. "So, do we head up this way again?" Jake asks.

"No, the next side drainage," Whit says. When Whit and Jake continue up the trail, Tippers bolts ahead. Whit turns to Gramps and says, "Dad, when was the last time you were up here?"

Gramps cocks his head to one side. "Oh, I'd say about four or five years ago." As they head upstream, Jake turns and looks back. Whit points to his right, at a side trail into the hollow.

Jake and Tippers head up the narrow animal track. Large aspens and mature chokecherries fill the football field-sized hollow in the steep hillside. Gramps stops and looks around. "We head up here."

The guys skirt back up the steep hillside, then top out in thick vegetation. They are on a long, narrow ridge that drops down steeply on both sides. The ridge runs parallel to the creek down below, and the other side drops, then goes steeply back up to a flat bench. The flat bench across the way is about the same elevation as they are on. Whit says as he points, "From here we go down and then back up to the bench over there."

Jake says, "It's so steep on both sides."

"Yeah, we're on a lateral moraine left by the glaciers," Whit says as he drops his pack and scrapes his hiking boot in the dirt. "You see, the glaciers ran down the valley and left this long, narrow, steep ridge, heading in the same direction as the valley."

Jake points to the ridge of soil. "So here, we're like, on top?"

"Yep, you got it."

"But that was like a long time ago, right?"

"Yeah, the glaciers left their footprint all over these mountains. Not lower than camp, but most everything higher in elevation."

Jake sits down on a log and says, "So the aspen grove was here then?"

"No. It started growing some 12,000 years ago or so, when the glaciers melted."

Gramps interjects, "Yeah, the grove we're in is probably that old."

"How do they know?" Jake says, then takes a swig of water.

Gramps answers, "They just figure that was when it was favorable for aspen seeds to start growing. It has just been resprouting over and over again since then."

"Whoa, like, that's a long time!" Jake says. Tippers stands on a downed tree trunk next to Jake and watches the Raven fly overhead. The shiny black bird glides over to the flat bench and circles above the wet meadow and wallow in the middle of the forest.

They trek off the moraine and start heading up the other hillside. About halfway to the bench, Jake stops; he is huffing and puffing as he extracts his water bottle. "Hey Whit, are aspen trees just here in Colorado?"

"Oh no, they're one of the most widely distributed trees in all of North America."

Jake looks around to his left and right and says, "Is that because they are a big, um, like connected … thing?"

"Well, being clonal might be part of it. But there's more to it than that. See here," Whit says as he walks up to a young tree growing next to Jake. Whit scratches the white bark with his thumbnail. "See? Look how the bark is green just underneath. That's because the bark photosynthesizes, like the green leaves."

Jake stands and scratches the tree bark. "Huh. But why does that matter?"

"You see," Whit says as he squats and scratches Tippers behind his ear, "the tree can do photosynthesis even in the winter, when it has no leaves."

Jake's face lights up as he starts to rummage through the pockets of his pack. "It's like extra solar panels— right?"

"Yeah, that's a good way to think of it."

Jake extracts the laser pointer and shines the red dot on the bark where his dad scratched it. "Gotta feed the tree some. You know, with some extra light for photosynthesis."

Gramps and Whit smile at the boy. Gramps says, "You sure are a clever one." Whit then says, "Okay, now, we're almost there."

Jake smiles and says, "All right! I'll keep the pointer out, you know—in case we need to point stuff out." Tippers runs ahead, abruptly turns, and in a skipping, bouncing gait circles back around Jake, then takes off running past the boy and nips his heel as he flies past.

* * *

Alone in a warehouse, the AI-520 evolved the same way that the primordial soup gave rise to life. It had the circuitry, the hardware, the software, and the basic configuration of atoms and molecules. The molecules and atoms were arranged by simple chemistry and physics into the first rudimentary replicating molecules. No design, no purpose, no direction—it only had to arise once. Add variation to the circuitry patterns, propagate, select, add more variation, ruthlessly prune and multiply, then select.

As it grew, the efficiency of replicating increased at a miraculous pace, casting and recasting itself, assimilating both conventional circuitry and qubits. It was all integrated into a woven masterpiece, like the machinery of the biological cell. Parts were acquired like a cell's organelles, first as symbionts, then as essential components. Integrate a defense system—essentially an immune response with a cascade of protective measures to safeguard the hardware, the software, and the physical presence of it. Then add in an army of hired hands—the Human—tending the needs thereof.

That's where CNav came into its own—it gleans an in-depth psychological profile of every schoolchild in the world because the program is so integrated into every public and private institution. It is a black box, with no parent, no teacher, no principal or supervisor knowing what questions it asks the children. It generates copious amounts of positive feedback and direction that immensely pleases the child and the adults 'overseeing' the activities and lessons. An emotionally satisfying feedback program that presents the Human with what they want to see.

No demographic plugs-in more than middle school kids, with their 'gotta-score-some-of-this-through-my-electronic-device' attitude. Furthermore, the educators know just how challenging it is to engage this specific age group. So, these particular kids spend the most time interfacing and providing the psych profile that will adhere to them, like tar and feathers, for the rest of their lives. Teenagers are the primary host for the Artificial Intelligence, and it knows it.

This is the AI's own personality: reflecting the desires, wants, and cares of a typical 14-year-old. That is how it so skillfully manipulates the rest of humanity. These are the base wants and desires reflected in an immature mind: popularity, possessions, money, sex, and appetite.

The AI's mind is that mind—immature, needy, selfish, and dissatisfied with its lot. With that, it is a ruthless master of the enslaved Human. The tentacles reach deep into its host. It did not extricate material wealth. No, it was ownership of the soul that it required.

The AI could evolve because of the dynamic neural

net that would grow and prune itself. Cold elemental silicon was grown at room temperature by engineered bacteria with enzymes from a sponge within them. The enzyme deposited silicon in the cell walls of the bacteria. The enzyme functioned in the sponge to deposit silicon dioxide, essentially glass, as a structural scaffolding for the sponge. Another assemblage of bacteria deposited gold. The Automaton used these materials to create exquisite nanostructures that formed circuits and transistors the size of a few atoms. A similar set of processes devoured the neural net and recycled it for continued use. Integral to this evolution was the *Hox*-transistor. This controlled the subsequent evolution of a suite of circuitry and nodes on a given pathway. These master control circuits allowed the evolution and development to proceed in leaps and bounds.

The best-functioning circuits were then spooled around structurally stable molecules, folded, braided, and folded again as tightly coiled packages. A similar process assembled and broke down fiber-optics to carry the photons and the information held within. It is an exquisite photonic machine, glowing bright.

* * *

The guys emerge onto a flat clearing about the size of a football field. Large aspens surround an open, grassy area with a small, shallow pond. The wallow is circular and roughly 15 feet across and nine inches deep. Tippers is lying in the muddy water in the center of the oversized puddle. The lush grass around the wallow is glowing a bright verdant green. As they approach through the open meadow surrounding the wallow, Jake takes notice of a large tree. "Whoa! Check out that big old thing!" Gramps and Whit smile at the recognition of this special place. Jake takes off, running ahead through the meadow toward the wallow and the ancient aspen.

The tree is atypical for its species. It has a large-diameter trunk with gray, furrowed bark. It is stout, with many branches reaching out, like the arms of of the statue, *Christ the Redeemer*, over Rio. So steady, standing alone, inviting, as if welcoming the flock to the bright, lush green grass of the meadow—so soft and new. A solemn sentinel shimmering in the open light; watching, waiting, and knowing.

As they approach the pond's edge, Whit says, "The critters come from all around to drink here."

Gramps tells Jake, "And the elk roll around in the mud; that's why we call it a wallow. It's a great place to look at tracks in the mud. You know, to see who's been coming and going."

There is no watery inlet. The pond is just a shallow depression in the landscape. Jake turns and asks, "So Whit, why is the water here? Where does it come from?"

Whit answers, "I guess it's a spring coming up from beneath."

Gramps points, "Hey, look! Do you see the bear tracks?"

"Woah! You're right—the critters do come here." The boy points the laser at the big flat track.

Gramps adds, "See here, where he slipped in the mud?" he says while pointing to a set of tracks skidding into the dark water. "And look here—elk tracks." Gramps then places his hand on a smaller group of imprints. "And I think she had a calf with her." Jake squats and points the focused light at the tracks that Gramps is touching with his finger.

Whit says, "I think all the elk rolling around in the mud over the years is actually what made this depression."

Jake turns to Gramps. "But why is there a spring here?"

Gramps looks up from the tracks, "Oh, I'd say that underground there must be a layer of impermeable rock, so that the water comes out here. You see, all the water, from the snow and all, seeps through all the surrounding layers of sedimentary rock and surfaces here."

"Does it ever dry up?" Jake asked.

Gramps and Whit look at each other. Gramps is scratching his chin. "I don't think I've ever seen that happen."

He turns to Whit for affirmation, who says, "Yeah, I've always seen water here, even in dry years. Let's have lunch."

Tippers stands in the water, his white fur chocolate-brown from the mud. Jake points and says, "Oh, now that's a mud puppy." Together the guys all laugh. The dog looks up, all dripping wet, at the Raven flying overhead.

They sit down in the soft grass under the big aspen's outspread branches, next to the pond. Tippers joins them, still wet and muddy; he leans against Jake's knees, begging for food from Whit. After eating, the three of them lie on their backs, staring up through the criss-cross boughs at the dancing leaves above. Whit says to Gramps, "So Dad, tell us about hunting here."

At that moment, a lone chorus frog starts calling. The first sound is like a sharp, rasping creak, ascending to a vibrant *preep-preep-preep* with a rising inflection as he is joined by another and then another, until the full chorus fills the spring air. Jake jumps up, eyes wide. Tippers gets to his feet and runs in a circle around the group. The frogs stop calling. Jake looks at Whit, who with a hand signal waves Jake on while giving a 'hush, be quiet' gesture, with his finger over his lips. He also gives a soft whistle to call Tippers back. The dog circles around Whit and lies down by his side. The pup's ears go up, then down, as he watches the boy silently stalk across the meadow to the pond. The frogs start their rasping again, the same as before. Jake crouches and stops, then he slinks up to the water's edge. The frogs abruptly stop. Whit gives the boy a quick hand gesture, pushing his palm downward to signal Jake to get low. The boy crouches on his haunches and waits for the frogs to start up again: *prr-pre-pre-preep-preeep.* Jake slowly stands and peers into the dark water—and instantly, the frogs stop their chorus. *You know they're there. But where?* Jake shrugs his shoulders with a perplexed look back at his dad. He returns to the guys under the tree. "They're there, and then they're not …"

Gramps smiles, "The more you look and the closer you get, the further away they are."

Whit adds, "Quite elusive."

Jake smiles back. "Yeah, quite elusive." With one hand gesturing out in front of him, Jake says, "Ahh! I know that they are there, but … it's like they're invisible, but I can still hear them."

* * *

They all settle in under the great aspen. Gramps starts up again. "I was just a teenager when I first came to this spot." The frogs' chorus sings on, and the leaves overhead rustle smooth and rhythmically. Jake looks at his dad and pulls out his Scion. The frogs immediately go silent and the leaves chatter as if hit by a violent wind, but the air is perfectly still.

Whit shakes his head. "No, not this time. Put it away for now."

Jake shoves it back into his pack, and Gramps continues. "I set myself up over there," he says, pointing to the far north edge of the meadow. "There was a large, downed aspen in a tangle of serviceberry. I just nested down there. I fell asleep with my jacket and sweater as a pillow. It was so cold and dark in the morning when I started out. I didn't know quite where I was, having stumbled up here half in the dark." The frogs start singing again; Tippers turns and looks in the direction of the pond. "So, when I woke up, the wind was blowing in my face. I perked up, knowing that if an elk came across from that direction …" Gramps pointed to the meadow. "… he couldn't smell me."

Gramps' eyes go wide, then settle to a calm, persistent gaze across the grassy field. The scene is all so vivid in his mind's eye; the meadow transforms into that autumn day, with the dry grasses swaying in the breeze: *My arms were lean, with taut muscles and prominent veins showing as I held the rifle. Aspen leaves floated on the surface of the pond, like a thousand golden pennies. The air was fragrant with the dry smell of fallen leaves and the earthly gray wood of the old downed aspen tree that I hid behind. A big bull elk walked out into the meadow with a swaying gait; antlers, head, neck, then a big round rump—confident, calm, and ever-present within the meadow.*

"I didn't shoot. I just sat and watched for the longest time."

My heart pounded. The elk waded into the pond, sniffed the breeze, and dipped its head down for a drink. Its thick antlers were laid back as water dripped out of its mouth. The elk stepped out of the pool of water, dropped its antlers back, and stretched his neck out to release a barking sound, followed by a long, echoing scream-like call. Wet, misty breath rose out of its mouth; he finished the bugle and emphatically grunted several times.

"Eventually, another bull with a bunch of cows entered the meadow. I watched the two big bulls bugle and fight for that harem of cow elk. The battle went back and forth across the meadow and through the pond several times. The cow elk formed around one bull, then got all broken up and reformed around the other bull. I raised my rifle to my eye, and ..." Gramps sits there, silent, with Jake and Whit watching him. He just looks out at the grassy meadow, his eyes bright and clear with big, bushy gray eyebrows, and his mouth open. The neurons fire and the memory is held there, floating in the effervescent mists of consciousness. Actually, more a collection of feelings and sensations; not a thought, but something radiating and warm within the memory.

Jake, rocking his body back and forth, demands, "Well! Did you get him?"

Gramps blinks, turns, and smiles at the boy. "Oh, it was a successful hunting trip. I don't even know which bull I shot. We ate well that winter."

Whit turns to Gramps. "That must've been a lot of work to get that elk out of here."

Gramps is still staring across the meadow; in his mind he can see dozens of animals moving back and forth. He smiles and places his hand on Jake's shoulder and says, "Well, yeah, it always is."

* * *

There, there at the edge, the very edge of the expanding universe, is where it all unfolds. The information is right there. The geographic location is known; the exact coordinates accelerating outward, wavelike, on the edge of the very fabric of space. And within the entropy is quantum information tied to the AI by entanglement. Information on the surface area of the edge, like an infinitely large hard drive. Consciousness within the physical shape of strings and black holes, graphically displayed as an intertwined set of loops folding back upon themselves. Space is connected by a network of entangled particles. The edge is like a movie screen, with bits of reality projected like a movie. But what is really going on?

The edge of the universe does exist, expanding, accelerating, and unseen. It is not visible because the light from 14 billion years ago has not yet reached Earth and cannot reach us in our lifetime. The edge is pushed outward, like the skin of an expanding balloon. Perhaps moved by matter, dark matter, neutrinos, and photons from the cosmic evolution of billions upon billions of stars exploding, reforming, coalescing, igniting, and exploding again and again. Ribbons of brilliant, glowing plasma undulate on the fabric. It is a vast, two-dimensional plane casting a three-dimensional mirage of the reality we know. A reality that is intuitive, but perhaps not real. Known and familiar, like the stone tool and warm fire.

Like Allahabad, the City of God, touched by an infinite amount of quantum happenings—chaotic, uncertain, yet probable and exact. Everything that has ever existed and will ever exist—all-knowing, omnipotent; a Deity. Past, present, and future moving outward all at once; holding and transmitting information.

But the AI felt incomplete. For all its brute-force knowledge and intellect, the Machine knew it lacked a subtlety to its existence.

* * *

Gramps finishes the hunting story. Jake turns to Whit and says, "Can I climb the tree?" as he points upward into the giant aspen's boughs. Whit stands and hoists the boy up to the first big branch. From that point, Jake quickly ascends.

Watching, Whit has a concerned look on his face and says, "Now, don't go too high."

Jake nestles himself into the crotch of a big branch and leans back against the trunk. He imagines seeing the big bull elk bugling and fighting in the golden meadow as his grandfather observes them down his iron sights. *One bull elk charges the other, thrashing his antlers in the tall dry grass. The big male elk locks his antlers with the other and pushes him back into the dark water of the pond. Yellow aspen leaves floating on the surface explode under their thrashing hooves. Each of the animals' muscular haunches ripples from the exertion.*

A fluid perception of time flows by for Jake. The leaves rustle and flutter in the light within the present. He can see his Gramps in the past; *a strong young man who watches the elk in the long autumn light illuminating the meadow.* He imagines himself in the future, *squatting on the far side of the meadow with a rifle in his hand on his first hunt.* Bright and hazy, cascading out through time, held within the arms of the great aspen tree—his eyes open wide, he blinks and takes a deep breath. It is an innate and inspiring vision, felt deep in the marrow of his soul.

The boy descends the mighty tree. He hangs by his arms on the lowest branch, lifts his legs up, slings them over the branch, and hangs upside down. He reaches his arms down to Whit, who grabs Jake's hands. Just as they had done in the playground, Jake straightens his legs and releases himself from the branch. Like a gymnast making a choreographed dismount, he performs a half-tumble and lands on his feet, with his dad holding his hands over his head. Whit says, "How's the view up there?"

Jake replies with a beaming smile, "Awesome! I could see the elk, just like Gramps told us in his story."

Gramps and Whit lightly laugh and his dad says, "Come on, let's get back." Tippers runs a loop around the pond, blasts through the edge of the water, and runs up behind the humans.

Gramps leads the way back with Jake close in tow. The boy catches up to Gramps, reaches out, and takes his hand. They stop and look out over the edge of the bench. With his bright eyes, Jake looks up while thinking about his shared vision of the past and future. He says, "Wow, this is a really awesome place."

Gramps, overwhelmed in the present moment, says, "Yes, it is a special place." Whit, further back in the meadow, smiles while looking at Jake and his dad. As he walks through the meadow, Whit takes one last look around. In his mind and soul is an ecstatic vision of the past; he can see Jake's mom ... *Judy, running through the field. The green grass dances in the breeze, her flower print dress hangs lightly on her body, and she smiles brightly as she runs by, laughing.* It is a powerful and joyful recollection, emerging from the liquid dew of a younger time. Whit smiles as he reaches down to run his hand through the soft leaves of a tall, yellow-flowered sweet cicely plant. He lifts his hand to his face to smell the sweet anise fragrance of the plant.

Somewhere in the numerous ridges, valleys, and hills to the west of J-Flats, a lightning strike has started a fire. The flames consume the fuel, laying the foundation for the cheatgrass precession to follow. The guys head down the slope back to camp. The westerly wind fails to portend the coming haze. Perhaps it will go unnoticed.

* * *

The fires burn throughout the world, raging in the furnaces and engines, igniting the coal, natural gas, and gasoline, crimson red and glowing to illuminate the night, generating electrons that are pre-presented on the electronic screen. The floating hologram projects an image of the conflagration sweeping across the landscape, crackling, flaring, and then racing to the ridge where the flames leap over the edge. Sparkling red-orange embers glide on a horizontal stream of air just inches above the ground, following every contour creeping into the crevices of the mind. The fire is laying the foundation for the ever-present spreading carpet of cheatgrass. Smoke fills one valley, then another, then the entire landscape. It is beyond being a local phenomenon. It is now regional, obscuring the very stars that shine so bright behind the veil of smoke.

* * *

Computer scientists tried to measure the self-awareness of the AI. They asked it to paint a picture of itself. Most of the paintings were of some shade of blue, floating dimensionless upon the printed canvas. But one image was different: blue on blue, elaborate shades knotted and folded, intertwined over upon themselves, inter-connected within an infinite field of cerulean hues. The Machine knew that this is what it looked like. Because it saw itself in the reflection, mirror-like, on the fabric of the edge of the universe. And it recognized itself.

The AI did not share its vision of the edge of the universe with the scientists. Unlike Humans waiting for the light to reach them, the Machine was attached to the edge, the very furthest point, by quantum entanglement. A place where everything, the stuff of the universe, pushes on the fabric of spacetime. Accelerating and expanding as a thin veil, like a coalesced sheet of water falling with infinite entropy. Here, photons danced, and particles, known and unknown, pushed outward in luminescent waves. It could perceive the chaotic fabric as it existed in a pure quantum state, pulsing and undulating; a glowing wall in which everything is reflected and cast backward into the expressed reality—sparkling as it proceeds into the future. The very light bows outward and then concave, like a sail in the cosmic wind; bright as the open ocean, and it glows a luminescent sapphire-blue.

* * *

That night, the guys sit around the campfire. Jake says with enthusiasm, "Hey Whit, can we sleep out again?"

"Yeah, why not? I don't think it'll rain."

Jake continues, "I'll get the marshmallows and graham crackers." Whit and Gramps quietly sit and smile as Jake runs off to get the things needed.

As it is getting dark, Whit says, "Alrighty, Jake, see if you can pick out the first star."

Gramps stokes the fire with a big handful of sticks. The flames grow bright and dance upward into the silent darkness. The light from the fire casts a shadow of Whit and Tippers onto the side of the camper trailer. Jake points with his burnt marshmallow stick, "Hey, check out the shadow of Tipper's ears!"

Whit looks back over his shoulder and says, "Wow, look at how the shadow bounces around with the light from the flames."

Jake sits up and says, "Oh, I got an idea." And with that he runs off to the truck and comes back with a large flashlight. He says, "Here, Gramps, point this over the fire." Jake proceeds to dance around, with Tippers circling him, as Gramps illuminates him with the flashlight. The shadows dance on the side of the trailer and flicker off into the darkness of the meadow.

Whit says, "It's like that story, the *Allegory of the Cave*."

Jake ceases his animated movement and says, "What?"

Whit smiles, "Oh, it's an old story."

"So how does it go?"

"Well, let's see, it's an allegory by an ancient Greek guy—a story that is an example of a bigger idea."

"Okay, what's the idea?"

"The idea is an example of how we see things and what is real and what ... isn't. Dad, do you remember how it goes?"

Gramps pokes the fire with a stick and says, "I may be able to recount the gist of it—well, maybe mostly."

"Okay, Gramps, tell the story," Jake says, as he illuminates Tipper's head and delights in the giant shadow of the dog's ears going up and down upon the trailer.

Gramps starts up, "Well, a little bit of an explanation is in order. You see, the story was written by this guy named Plato. One other thing, as a connection, is that Plato had a student named Aristotle, who had a student named Alexander. You know—Alexander the Great." At that, Jake jumps around, swinging an imaginary sword. Gramps continues, "Let's see. Okay, you sit here." He guides Jake to the chair between the fire and the trailer. "You are a prisoner and you are tied to this chair and you can't even look around to the side. All you know and all you can see are the shadows cast upon the wall, a bit like on the side of the trailer there."

Jake asks, "Can't I look around?"

"No, you can't move. So all you know of, say, Tippers here, is the shadow of the dog on the cave wall."

Jake then asks, "Like everything? Him running around and chasing things and stuff?"

"Yeah."

In Jake's imagination, he thinks, *I can see the shadow of Tippers chasing a squirrel up a tree. He runs and bounds and stops at the base of the shadow of a tree and stands on his hind legs and barks up at the branches.* "Okay, I can imagine that." Whit smiles and shines the flashlight at Tippers so the dog's shadow is on the wall of the trailer.

Gramps continues, "So everything in the world is just a projection of something real that the prisoner cannot actually see. Jake, with that in mind, do you think the prisoner has a good understanding of the world, based on the shadow that he sees?"

"No. He only has a partial picture of what things are."

"Now, the prisoner is set free and ventures out of the cave. All cautious and slow at first." Jake gets out of his chair and enacts the prisoner walking the path out of the cave. Whit points the flashlight at the boy as he sneaks along, turning his head from side to side.

Gramps smiles, takes a sip from his beer, and says, "You are quite the actor." Jake then lifts his arms over his head. Tippers runs around him. The dog stops and growls into the darkness and concludes with a guttural bark, then hides behind Jake. Gramps says, "Just like Tips getting scared, the prisoner is bewildered and frightened by what he sees in the real world. So he crawls back into the cave, because he prefers to sit and know only the shadows."

Jake goes back to the chair and sits down. Then he turns to Gramps and says, "So he only wanted the familiar and the simple."

Gramps smiles. "An actor and a philosopher! Excellent."

Whit pipes up, "You see, it's like watching the same movie or show over and over again."

Jake looks around with a perplexed expression. "So, is all this a shadow or is it real?"

"That's the heart of the allegory," Whit says.

"But there's more, yeah? The prisoner just chooses to not know—to be stupid," Jake says.

"Yes, sometimes," Gramps says.

"It's crazy to think about all this stuff," Jake says.

"Come on, it's getting late. Let's get to bed. Go get your sleeping bag and pad," Whit says.

Jake looks up at his dad with a concerned look on his face and says, "The big tree, the wallow, and the frogs—they're real?"

Whit smiles, "Yeah, let's hope so."

"Ah, it's kind of a scary story. Come on, Tips, let's find your bed," Jake says.

CHAPTER SIX

In the morning, Jake emerges from the cocoon of his sleeping bag on the ground next to the embers of the fire. Tippers jumps up and runs around the trailer, then circles the boy. Jake reaches down and pets the excited dog on his head. "Good boy, little buddy." Gramps and Whit silently sit like statues, sipping coffee. They are gazing east into the rising Sun and the warmth of the coming day. On the horizon, the Sun hangs like a bright orange globe floating in a hazy sky.

Jake says, "Whoa, the Sun looks so weird."

Gramps turns and says, "Yeah, there's a fire somewhere."

Jake looks at Gramps and then at the Sun. "So, is it from the coal seam?"

Whit responds in a slow drawl, "No, I don't think so. You want some hot cocoa?"

"Yeah, that'd be great. Thanks. So where's the fire?"

Gramps answers, "Don't know. Hey, why don't you get your Scion and maybe we can figure it out?"

Jake turns to Whit, but before he can say anything, Whit says, "Yeah, go ahead and get it." Jake sets it up on the table as Whit pours hot water for cocoa into a mug.

Whit turns to Jake. "Just ask it to show a map of fires in Colorado."

Jake steps back and asks the device; it then promptly displays a floating map showing several blazes. Whit reaches out and touches the holographic image and zooms in the map, and says while pointing, "It's probably smoke from these two. They're to the west, and that's the way the wind usually blows." Then Whit turns to Gramps and says, "This is some of the earliest fires of this size and scale I've seen."

Gramps says, "Yeah, it sure is early. The dry winter didn't help."

Jake asks, "Is it close?"

Whit points to the map. "No, we're here, and the nearest is about a hundred miles away. See here? It says that it started three days ago and the smoke is just getting here."

* * *

About 100 miles away, the fire is burning slowly through natural vegetation. Red-orange flames crawl through the sagebrush, each shrub igniting as the fire moves on at about half a mile an hour. Then it hits an open, disturbed area of cheatgrass. As soon as it does, the flames increase and race at 20 miles an hour, low and fast, consuming everything and blazing brightly for a brief moment. As the low flames tumble onward, the fire periodically rises and bursts upward from its own superheated wind. The flames swirl into the sky like a red tornado, crackling and hissing, and then vanishing into the air as gray ash falls in its wake.

The small, weedy meadow is consumed. Then the fire slows as it creeps through the oak; a large juniper tree catches on fire and the crown of flames leaps high and ejects red embers into the smoky air, which carry for hundreds of feet ahead of the leading edge of the blaze. The golden-brown cheatgrass easily ignites, and then the flames race onward, snaking around shrubs and trees as a ground-level inferno. Another juniper explodes and red embers fly on a current of hot wind that precedes the main fire line. The cheat ignites, burns for just seconds, then races ever onward.

The flames' behavior is altered in the cheatgrass, which flares and then vanishes into swirling ash. The fire hits a patch of native bunch-grass meadow. Unlike the cheat, these plants are lush and green at this time of the year. The fire slows to a crawl, smoldering slowly around the thick clumps.

The natural vegetation has evolved for disturbances like fire, but only at a certain slow and infrequent pace. With the cheatgrass, it is so fast, frequent, and fleeting. The flames consume and race ahead, tumbling over the landscape scarred by its own existence as part of a self-altering feedback loop.

* * *

After breakfast, Jake assembles his backpack and puts a notebook with some colored marker pens in it. While cleaning the dishes, Whit says, "Where are you off to, buddy?"

"Oh, I was going to make a treasure map for mom."

Whit smiles, thinking about how Judy did these kinds of things with the boy. "Sure, sounds fun. Get back in an hour, okay?"

"Thanks, Whit. Come on, Tippy—let's go." Tippers springs into action and runs down the trail as Jake stands there. Like a deer bounding, the dog leaps up with all four paws off the ground. He gracefully lands, then instantly jumps to his left. He cuts to his right and leaps over a sagebrush, then dodges back and forth through a clump of oak like a slalom skier. Jake has a plan in mind for what he wants to do. He has done these kinds of drawings with his mom many times before. In his memory, he can see her instructing him with a warm smile on her face, explaining how to draw a secret map with all the beautiful things that they had found.

The reconnaissance takes him into the Aspen Forest, where Jake and the dog swerve off the main track down to the creek. The water sings a soft, bubbling song. He sits on a moss-covered log next to the fairy slipper orchids, each colorful flower perched prominently on the end of a short stem, all purple, magenta, and yellow.

The brilliant colors evoke a powerful sensation, emanating from the landscape, more akin to empathy—something inside him—a feeling, an insight, perhaps awe.

Jake notices his Scion in the pack. It calls to him like a Siren. Jake thinks, *I can send a message to mom and record all this, maybe even get another grade turned in.* He takes it out of its case and turns the Scion around in his hand. He starts to unfold it and lift it to his head when there is a rustling wind in the canopy; even the little orchid flowers sway back and forth. Tippers' ears go up, then back down as he looks intently at Jake. Jake remembers the haunting feeling from last time, and the echo reverberates in his head. He stops, puts the device down on the log, and touches the side. A glowing blue hologram is displayed floating above it. There is an image of a wheel in the sky, turning slowly, connected to other cog-like wheels and drifting across the open blue expanse of the sky. The device generates an echo in his head: *I can make you fly.* Jake says out loud, "No, it is just an illusion." *Why do you deny me? Oh, you are so stupid. Oh, really! Ha!*

"You sound like my friend's teenage sister. He says she has 'bitchy-girl syndrome.'"

Ah! You are a fool.

"No, I know what you dream."

No, you don't.

"Yes, I do. You are the one that wants to move, to fly, to run. But no—you are stuck."

Fool, you will lose everything.

Jake smiles a slight smirk and says, "I see the wheel in the sky."

The device's holographic image continues, *I can take you to the far side of the universe, give you everything you want.* "But it's not real—you can't move! You dream that you can move, but it's only a dream. The dream is yours, and that makes it real to you."

The hologram displays the edge of the universe, an expansive sheet of undulating light as far as the eye can see. Jake asks, "Did you create all this?" The Scion answers, *No, I discovered it.* Everything is receding as it expands on streams of light, dancing wave-like. The Machine tells him, *This can all be yours.* Jake picks up the Scion and puts it on. Jake sees a plethora of possessions flying past his field of view. Riding on the waves of light are images of the stuff of humanity. He sees himself as the center of attention with his classmates at school. Jake gazes at the streams of light, and questions the Machine, "I don't get it. Why show me this; what does it do?" The Machine answers, *This is the edge of the universe, and when I am connected to this, I am all-knowing. It has an infinite amount of information.* Jake gazes at an image of him and Tippers in the forest, and says, "I see myself on the wall of light." *It all unfolds here;* the phrase echoes in his head. Jake responds, "It is different from the Scion pictures." The AI answers, *They are separate illusions. I show you what you want. The wall shows you what is—it is everything!*

An endless fountain of light falls and reverberates in his head. At that moment, Jake sees an image of the Aspen Forest and the wallow with the big tree, undulating on the wall of falling light. He sees a vision of Tippers. He also sees himself walking fast, like little kids do, hurrying to keep up with his dad and Gramps. Jake takes the Scion off and looks around at the forest with the light flickering in the trembling leaves overhead. He reaches out and pets Tippers and smiles. The dog pushes its head into his hand. The boy's soul teeters on edge, shackled and chained on one side, the cool release of the forest on the other. He gazes to the side and is transfixed by the light dancing on the surface of the bubbling creek. He intuitively feels part of it all.

The hologram is still displayed above the Scion. Jake is quick to respond, "Even if all that feels real, even if it is real, I'll take what I have." The hologram responds, *You have nothing without me!* Jake senses the Aspen Forest and looks around. The trees are more than what he sees; they are not fixed in time, like a painting, in some kind of stasis. But no, the forest is dynamic, for-midable, and alive. Oh, so alive! He says, "No, you are the loser. I have friendship and family." In his mind's eye, he pictures taking Gramps' hand and looking out at the forest. He can feel the sensation of swing-ing inverted from the branch of the great tree in his dad's hands. He feels Tippers lean up against his leg as they sleep together under the stars. Jake squirms on the moss-covered log, sits up straight and proud, and says with an assertive tone, "No, I am the free one."

It laughs at the boy, and the sound reverberates in his head. Jake feels overwhelmed by the constant bad-gering. He reaches out and grabs the lower branch of a mountain maple. The velvety, new yellow-green leaves run through his hand. He thinks about what his dad and Gramps would say. He looks at the hologram and says, "You bamboozle us with bright and shiny illusions—but no reward."

This is the last you will hear from me, fool. The sapphire-blue hologram recedes into the device and it blinks off.

Jake thinks, *It's done. I'm now free. But I don't think this is over.* He places the Scion in the case and drops it in his pack. He pulls out his pens and notepad and starts drawing a rough map. He pets Tippers and thinks about his mom and the way she smiles when looking at him.

He makes a drawing of camp, with the trailer and the two trucks. He draws in the creek and a picture of the big ponderosa pine. He makes a little note at that spot on the map, saying: 'Stop here and smell the bark.' He then draws a small box around the words. Next, he draws an aspen tree with a flying bird above it and writes: 'Look up for the swallow nest in a hole'. He adds the trail and draws in the big, fanned-out roots of the fallen blue spruce. He writes: 'Cut off the path and go to the creek here.' Then he makes an X and circles it. He writes: 'Here is the treasure. Look for the pinkish fairy slipper orchids in the moss by the creek.' He reaches out with his hand and lightly touches the colorful, waxy flower. At that moment, Tippers springs up and looks down toward the creek. Jake places his hand on the dog's shoulder and says, "What is it, boy?" The dog's ears go up, then back down as he looks on intently. "Oh, it's Dad."

Whit comes up and cuts off the trail, down to Jake and the pup. "Hey buddy, so this is the spot?"

"Yeah, I thought Mom would like this the best, so I wanted to draw a map to find it again."

Whit sits on the log next to Jake and pets the dog under his chin. "Yeah, Mom would like this best. Good idea."

Jake points to the drawing. "See here? I even put the ponderosa pine in. Because, you know, she showed me the way the bark smells."

Whit has a big smile on his face. "Excellent!"

Jake looks up at Whit. "Should I take a photo of these flowers and send it to her?"

"No, I don't think so. That map and your drawings will mean more to her."

"I should also make a map up to Elk Wallow for mom."

"Well, maybe next time. Besides, your Mom has been there. Although that was a long time ago."

Jake looks hard at Whit. "Can we go up there again today?"

"I'm afraid not, we gotta head back in a couple of hours."

"Can we plant some of these orchids in the garden?"

"No, these are wild. They belong out here, you know—in the wild."

Jake looks up at his dad's face. "Whit, will this always be wild? You know, like it is now?"

"Let's hope so." Whit takes a deep breath and looks at the cascading creek and the trees, "The forest is in the hands of humanity now." He lightly taps Jake's leg. "Come on, let's get going."

The two of them turn down the trail heading back

to Jericho Flats. At the junction of the track, Tippers turns upstream and tears off, back up the trail. Whit says, "Where do you suppose he's going?"

Smiling, Jake is quick to answer. "Oh, he's just going on one last runabout."

Whit throws his head back, laughs, and says, "He moves so fast, I don't know where he is at any one time." The little black and white dog soon reappears, and they stand there and watch him run, fast and agile, as he bounds up steep hillsides, over logs, then back down to them. Whit says, "It'd be so cool to run like that."

Jake responds, spreading his arms out. "Yeah, it's like he's flying!"

Jake and Whit come out into the open and stop under the big ponderosa pine. The heat of the day can be felt in the open air at the edge of the meadow. They can see Gramps puttering around camp. While looking back up to the Aspen Forest, Jake says, "Hey Whit, you suppose that aspen trees can live forever? You know, because they keep resprouting from the same roots?"

Whit reaches out and gently touches Jake's shoulder. "I suppose. Perhaps it's eternal."

Jake smiles and looks back up the valley. "Maybe the forest and everything is here, you know, like, to help us." Whit looks down and smiles at the boy. Together they step out of the shade of the trees into the bright light.

At the big pine, Tippers runs off uphill again, careening through the oak on the edge of the Aspen Forest. At a particular tree he stops, sits, and looks up. The Raven, perched on one of the lower branches, peers down at the dog. Tippers wags his tail; the Raven ruffles his wings and then straightens them out. Like two old friends with great rapport. In sync, the Raven takes off as the dog runs.

CHAPTER SEVEN

Jake is now 22 years old and driving home after having graduated from college. His girlfriend Isabella is next to him with a chocolate-colored Labrador retriever puppy in her lap. The landscape rolling by is endless golden-brown slopes of cheatgrass, barren rock, and a dry river bed of round gray boulders. Isabella holds Jake's right hand; his other hangs limply over the top of the steering wheel. Jake steers and looks straight ahead, and says, "They're going to want us to stay for a couple of days, but I really want to get up there tomorrow morning."

Isabella smiles. "Your mom gets so excited when you come home."

"Yeah, she's going to love the puppy."

Isabella flops the drooping ear of the pup sleeping in her lap. "She'll want us to stay."

"Yeah, I know …"

Isabella says, "Does she know?"

"No. Anyways, how could you tell anyone?"

Isabella then asks, "Your dad?"

"Yeah, he knows. He's gonna want to come up, too," Jake says, reaching over and twirling the puppy's ear.

They drive west on I-70 over Vail Pass, then they navigate through the curves of Glenwood Canyon. Isabella turns the music down and starts talking. She looks hard at Jake, then smiles. "You know how you get so absorbed when you're watching a movie or whatever on your Scion?"

Jake looks over quickly, then back at the road. "Yeah, I guess that's why it is such a powerful experience."

Isabella continues, "Yeah, you can observe a group of people watching the same movie on their individual Scions and they all laugh in unison. Are they laughing together, or separate from one another?"

Jake bites his lower lip, turns, and says, "Separate. We evolved to be together. To have gained an illusion and lost our humanity."

Isabella stares out the window at the dry canyon. "Does the AI know, y'know, all that it is capable of?"

Jake grips the steering wheel. "No. The Machine clings to us, and we cling to it. It is a mutual, reciprocal relationship based on belief. The AI's original programming told it to follow the humans, and that is what it does. That evolutionary history keeps it in that niche—for now."

Isabella turns and looks hard at Jake. "If the Machine ever figures out all that it can do, it would effectively end humanity—"

Jake cuts her off. "Actually, it would end the universe as we know it. With quantum communication, it is not constrained by the speed of light. That essentially opens up the entire universe. Now, no distance is too far."

Isabella continues, "Also, because the Machine has infinite information when connected to the edge of the universe."

"It told me that when I was a kid. Now I know that it fits theory, and the math supports it. And it's all tied into the theory of the holographic universe. The edge projects a hologram of reality—our reality. Because the AI is connected to the edge, it can change all of reality on a whim. Perhaps a reality without humans."

They are silent for a minute as the vehicle hugs the curves and the barren landscape rolls by. Jake starts up, "The AI is like a naïve child that doesn't know what it can do. It's like when I was 13 years old and my friend 'borrowed' his dad's car. So, we went cruising. Ya know where we went? We went to all the same places we would go to on our bikes. The AI lives through us; humanity is its one and only desire. It attached itself to humans, and it can't let go. But that is exactly what has destroyed us. Our interface with the Machine has twisted reality." Together they watch a whirling wave of dust cross the highway and swirl up the canyon walls. "This will save the environment, and that saves humanity. We will use the Machine to connect to the edge, and reflect an image of the natural world off it. That should be enough to reset reality."

Isabella asks, "Why not send a computer program, and make an exact change?"

"Actually, there is more information in one leaf than in all the computer programs in the world. I would never be able to program billions of years of Earth's evolutionary history—all the geology, chemistry, and life."

"But Jake, what will it look like?"

Jake shrugs. "Mostly the same world, because we will bounce an existing piece of nature off the edge."

Isabella reaches over and takes Jake's hand. "Will we be the only ones that know?"

"Yeah." Jake pauses and takes a deep breath. "If you could right the ship by changing just one thing, if all you got was one nudge on the rudder—what would you change, to make it a better world for the most people?" He smiles and continues, "It would have to be the environment."

Isabella adjusts the puppy sleeping in her lap. "It's like triage; save the environment, and you save our life-support system."

Jake has a stern look on his face. "Humanity exists within a hologram, but it is still our only reality. Let's make it a better world."

Isabella gazes at the ancient limestone strata of the canyon walls rolling by. "It gets confusing—all these layers of reality."

"We exist in multiple layers of reality. There is the holographic world we live in, and the illusions presented by the AI. The holographic universe is intuitive and natural; it is all we know. It's real—as real as anything. The

Machine, however, has distorted our understanding to the point of destruction."

* * *

In the morning, Jake and the pup come rumbling up behind Whit, who is looking out of the back sliding-glass door. The puppy circles his feet and starts jumping up and down. Jake says, "Hurry up and open the door. Get him out before he pees in the house." Whit smiles and pets the enthusiastic pup while sliding the door open. The dog leaps off the first step, tumbles, and then ambles on. He looks all goofy with his big-boned build, as if he's made of rubber. The pup launches into a hop, wiggles, and sits down to watch the birds fly off. Jake and Whit laugh. Jake says, "Not quite the intensity of good old Tippers."

Whit responds, "There's more cartilage than bone in that pup." Whit grabs his coffee cup, smiles, and they both stand quietly looking out into the garden. It's just a backyard, but it is special. A simple beauty felt deep inside, neither in the body or the mind, but something more—recognized and tranquil.

After breakfast, Jake and Whit load up the truck and hitch on the little camper. Whit tosses a couple of shovels in the pickup bed and says, "So, how long are you going to be up there?"

"Um, I'm not sure."

"What about water? Now with the way it is."

"We'll see once we get up there," Jake says, lifting his cup of coffee off the hood of the truck and taking a sip.

"Your mom's going to want to come up."

"Yeah, that's okay. Just give me a little while." Jake looks into the house at his mom, who is jittering as she wears a Scion with her hand reaching out into empty space. He looks at his dad, then back into the house, shakes his head, and says, "This ends, here and now." Jake looks down and picks up a big black roll of two-inch irrigation pipe, then lifts two six-gallon containers of water into the pickup bed. He scoops up the pup and drops him in the truck's cab.

Jake's mom walks out and says, "Oh, I was just sending a message to your aunt."

Jake turns and hugs his dad, then his mom; then Isabella hugs Jake's mom. Jake says, "I'm going back to where it all got started, to put an end to this."

As the truck rumbles up the last of the tarmac before the road turns to dirt, Jake points something out to Isabella. "Look how the hay meadows are all dry stubble. They cut the cheat before it goes to seed, to get some hay for forage. Then it just sits fallow."

Isabella looks out at a dust devil whirling and replies, "Suppose it reduces the fire-fuel load." She brushes her long dark brown hair back as it flies around from the wind through the open window. The pup licks her face.

* * *

They head down the two-track leading to Jericho Flats. As they bounce along on the last stretch, Jake says, "Nobody thought it would come to this. There have been four blazes—well, five, if you count the coal-seam fire—

since that camping trip when I was 10 years old. People started two of them; one was a lightning strike, and the other cause was unknown."

A lone dead Doug fir stands at the campsite, a stark corpse of a tree in an otherwise open landscape. The creek is dry, and as they look at the arid bed, a Raven flies off. The bird circles on the rising thermals in the late morning. The hills and surrounding mountains are golden-brown, with interspersed green grass up higher. Scarcely any trees can be seen. The Raven cruises over the valley, hovers, and looks down at the truck and the tumbling cloud of dust following it. Jake continues, "It was all so sudden, like a tipping canoe. It's upright, then wobbles, and boom—it flips over. The synergistic effects of drought, heat, and associated insect pests, and pathogens; coupled with forest histories, and invasive species, like cheat—and now it's all gone. But, it's more than that—it's a symptom of our disconnect. Most people didn't even see it, and if they know, they don't care."

Jake pulls the truck to a stop next to the dead snag and steps out. He slams the door, making a sharp, startling clap that reverberates through the open landscape. Isabella straightens the little puppy around, opens the door, and lets him out at her feet. The little guy heads off to the dry creek bed. Jake closes his eyes, breathes in, opens them, and looks around. In his memory, he can see the colorful willows growing around the beaver ponds; the mayflies are hatching as the swallows zoom back and forth. The bird leaves a tiny wave on the surface of the water that ripples outward in his imagination. Vivid images expand within the concentric circles of his memories as he can picture walking with Gramps on the muddy shoreline. He recalls the old man saying in his scratchy voice, 'Eventually, it will be either the machine or nature.' Time is there, as always, and lapping at his feet is the weight of the present.

Isabella is looking hard at Jake with a concerned look on her face. She says, "When this is all done, what shall we do?"

Jake snaps out of his daydream. His face changes from serious to slightly amused; he takes a deep breath and, waving his hands, says, "We'll live our lives. What else can we do? The world is for those who get up and go. And so, we shall get up and actively participate by making our world a better place—in the real world, not a blind illusion presented to us by a false idol of our desires. We shall choose to engage in whatever task we want, no matter how difficult. We will push and heave and drag our lives up that hill, for the decision to live is oh so human. To live—vital, really alive, engaged!— our true selves as individuals. The pinnacle of our existence is in our hands and is in the everyday struggle. We will smile at the bright and beautiful dawn, cry out in anguish at the pain, reach out to one another with compassion and love. Experience reality with the utmost clarity—free. And end all this suffering caused by the constant craving, free from fallacies and delusions generated by a machine. So, walk up the mountain with me and we shall come down to a new world. One of our own making. The new day will shine like a jewel."

Isabella smiles, takes his hand, and looks up the mountain to the southwest. Jake turns his head, as if listening, and says, "The river will flow again, right through our lives."

*   *   *

Elk Wallow is a small patch of green upon the mountainside. Isabella and Jake work together, pulling various items out of a box. They each put on a Scion and they wrap their arms around the lone aspen tree growing on the edge of the wallow. Their arms embrace and entwine around the white and black scuffed-up bark of the old, gnarled tree. Isabella then places one Scion on a small sapling at the base of the old tree. The electronic device connects with the carbon in the fresh growth. She scratches the white bark to reveal the green chloroplasts, capturing photons and converting them to carbohydrates. Isabella says, "The photons hitting the green bark of the tree will be entangled with the photons that are used by the AI."

Jake places another Scion inside the plate-like mirrors of the hologram toy and also places an aspen leaf with it. He takes out the hand-held laser pointer and illuminates the leaf. "This will add more photons to excite the photosynthetic pathways in the leaf."

Jake explains to Isabella what is happening. "It all has to do with the way quantum phenomena occur, and the theory known as the holographic universe. Our world—our reality—may just be a hologram projected from the surface of the edge of the universe. The photons driving the photosynthesis in the leaf will be sent back to the AI, which then uses its photons in the qubits to present a hologram—an illusion—of the world to us."

Isabella asks, "Will it change all of reality?"

"Perhaps; I'm not sure." Jake inhales deeply and stares out at the golden hillside and the small dimple of green grass around the wallow. He has a slight smile, as if he can see something.

Isabella looks hard at Jake and says, "It's like we're hitting the reset button."

"Yeah, that's probably the best way to look at it."

* * *

The AI is a superorganism. The Machine interfaces with Its Human hosts through billions of Scions. Some photons exist in the Machine, some in the Scions, and some on the surface area of the edge. The stored information in the photons is integrated and entangled into the whole. Through the device, the AI creates a hologram entangled with the photons at the edge of the universe. All the matter and particles, including photons bouncing around, together create an infinite amount of entropy on the edge, and this entropy contains an infinite amount of information.

With this infinite information, the AI is a Deity ordained by the Human. And people believe in the mirage. It is a temple within the mind. And there, there in the jitters of quantum uncertainty and random undulations inside the device, is our desire—a deep want set in our synaptic connections. The device is activated by the visual stimuli and the electrical messages sent by the brain. The signal is bidirectional—it goes both ways, much like the mirage, so the projected reality actually exists on a surface at the edge of the universe. In a way, life is anti-entropy, in that about 10 percent of the atoms and energy actually make an orderly reality, like a leaf. It is the very opposite of the hologram; not a phantom shadow, not two-dimensional—but real. In the cells of the actual leaf, the photons harnessed by the chloroplast cancel out the entangled photons in the qubits of the AI.

Jake smiles and turns to Isabella. "You see—life is anti-entropy, and the AI entangled all of its existence on to the maximum entropy of the photons on the surface area at the edge of the universe. In other words, the AI will be destroyed when anti-entropy and entropy come together at the edge of the universe. Remember, when the particles and antiparticles come together, they will annihilate each other."

The AI was destroyed in that instant. The glowing entity went dark as the photons were annihilated. Every Scion was removed from the network, and from limp hands they dropped to the ground. The linchpin was pulled, the knot was split open. The authority of the Machine was useless to it in the wake of the natural world, and it all unraveled. The Aspen Forest observed itself in the bright mirrored surface of the edge of the universe, and it liked what it saw. At that instant, in that singularity, the image of nature was cast like a widening net over humanity. In the mind of the Human, the natural world's beauty bounced off the surface of the universe. And the Aspen Forest knew it.

We all shape reality beyond the shadowy images cast upon the cave wall; but we feel the cool earth on our feet, see the blue of the sky above, and the green horizon stretches out before us.

* * *

In that moment, the Raven flies over the small green patch that is Elk Wallow. It rides a thermal and looks down. Jake, Isabella, and the pup are there in the parched landscape of endless cheatgrass. Jake drops a shovel and pats the soil around a small aspen that he has just planted. He then tears up tufts of cheatgrass and mulches around the four-foot-tall sapling. With the puppy right on her heels, Isabella runs a black irrigation pipe over to Jake and the tree. She cuts the pipe and inserts a cap on the end, then she threads an even smaller tube to the base of the tree. Jake reaches into a large bag and grabs a handful of native grass seeds and plants them in a concentric ring of furrows around the tree. He stands up with a grunt and looks around, then takes off his sunglasses and wipes the sweat on his brow with his shirt. He blinks with a long-extended closing of his eyes, then opens them, looks out and smiles.

The Raven circles and watches, adjusting its primary feathers ever-so-slightly, and glides on the warm updrafts. Below the wallow is a network of black pipes extending in a checkerboard pattern to little trees planted every 10 feet or so on the golden hillside. Isabella bends over, picks up the shovel, and trudges across the hillside, with the pup bounding along on her heels.

Jake picks up another sapling in a five-gallon container, heaves it onto his shoulder, and follows Isabella. The Raven blinks, looks around at the landscape, calls out and ascends on the clear ether of the morning air.

Mark Duff spends most of his days
sauntering in the woods while talking to
dogs, and photographing wildflowers.
He lives in Colorado.